Enchanted foot

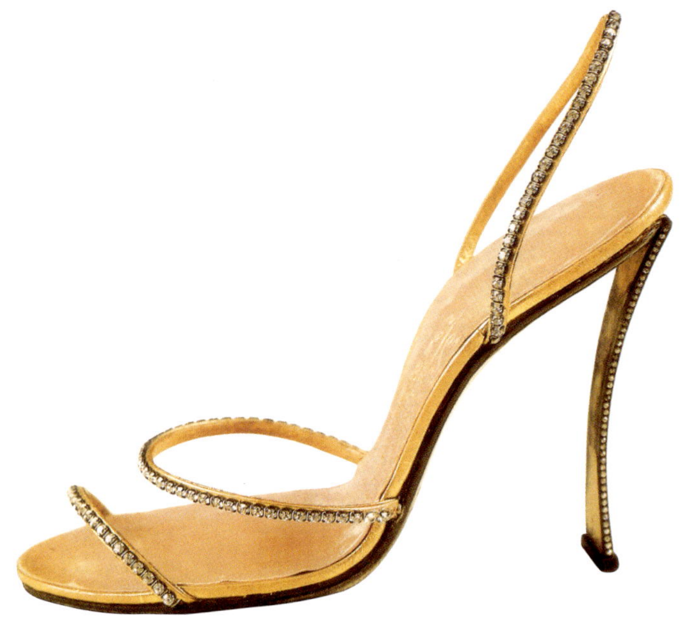

Publishing director:
Jean-Paul Manzo

Texts by: Hans-Jürgen Döpp

Designed: by: Sébastien Ceste

Publishing Assistant: Maria Muhle

Photographic credits

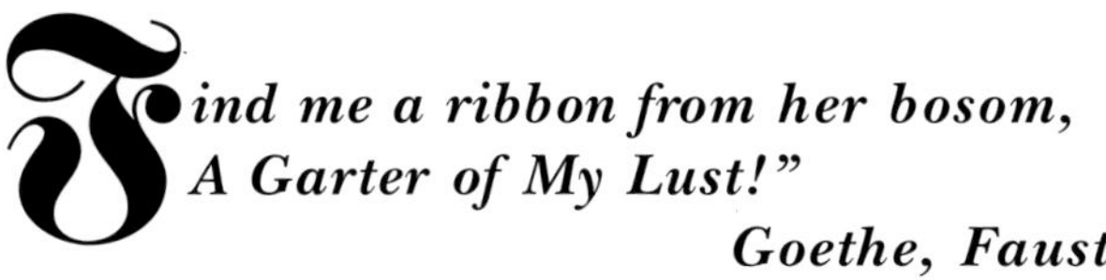

"Find me a ribbon from her bosom,
A Garter of My Lust!"
                    Goethe, Faust

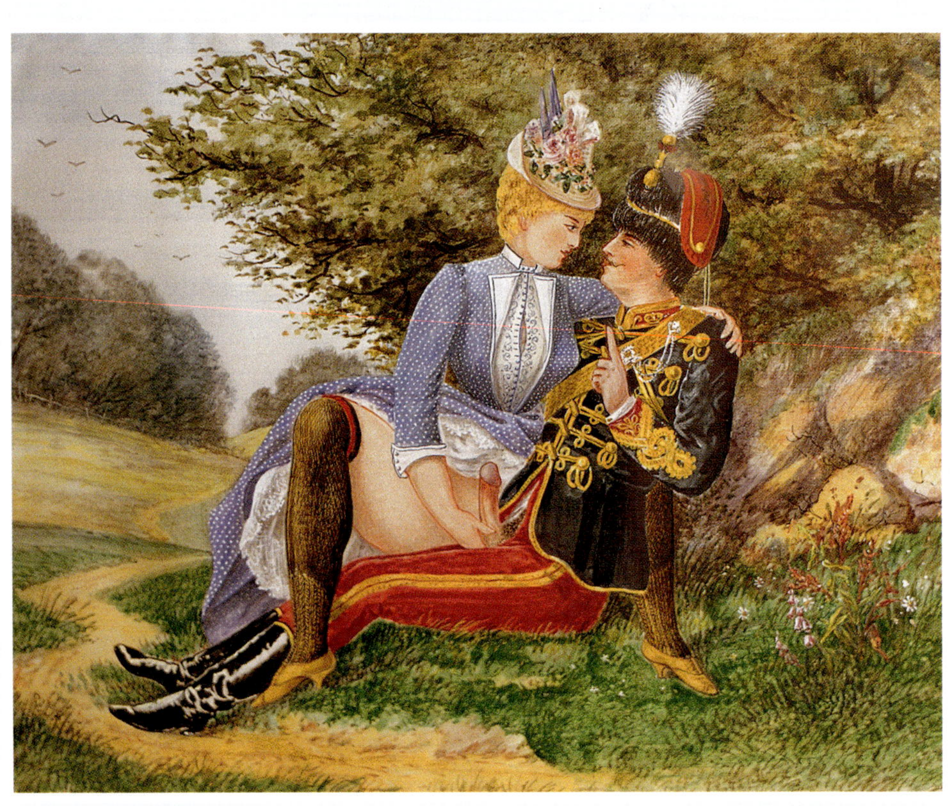

1. Watercolour, from an English notebook, 1880.

$\mathcal{E}$very lover is also somewhat of an erotic fetishist. He or she loves objects that have been in close or intimate contact with the beloved and thus are especially dear. These objects ensure the proximity and closeness of the beloved. Special physical forms of expression of this desired person could also become a symbol for the significance of the partner as a loved and cherished individual: a way of walking, a way of smiling, "the way you wear your hat, the way you sip your tea." Physical characteristics such as hair color, shape of eyes and mouth, clothing, etc. can constitute the cause, the movens, of being in love. Today, a value such as youth itself seems to have turned into an overvalued fetish.
As long as these concrete and physical symbols represent the totality of the loved individual, one can speak of a "normal fetish".

* «la façon dont tu portes ton chapeau, la façon de boire ton thé».

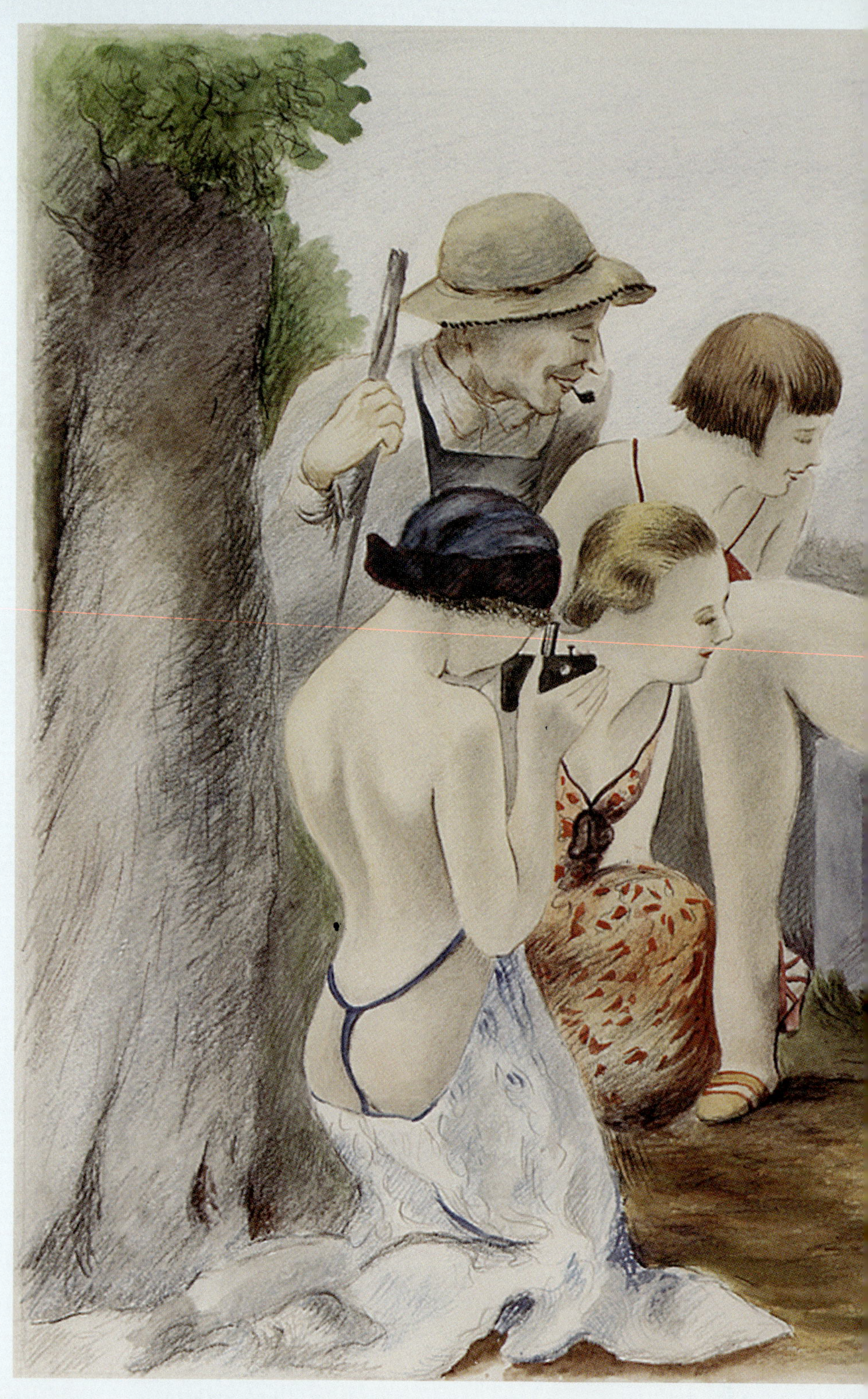

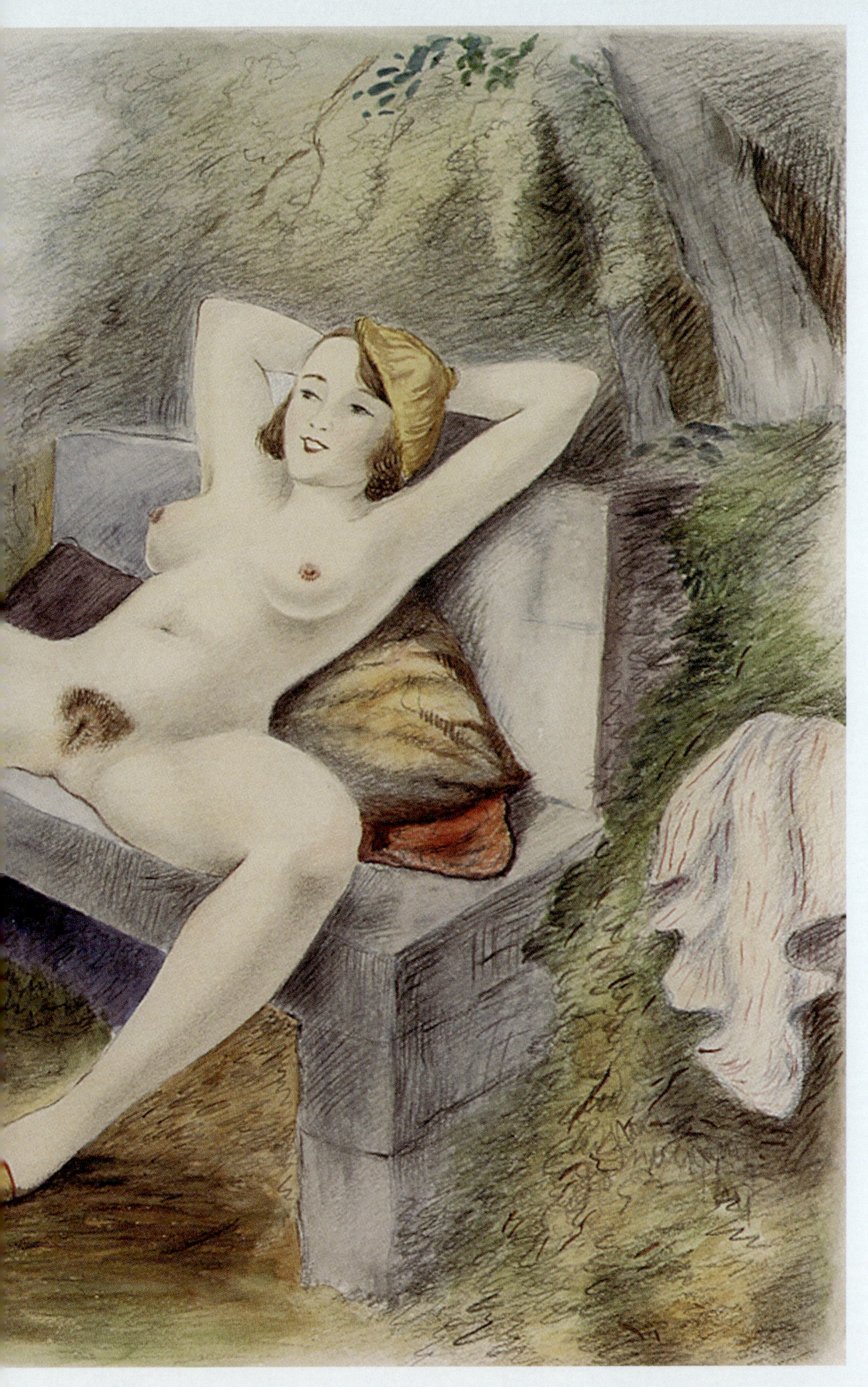

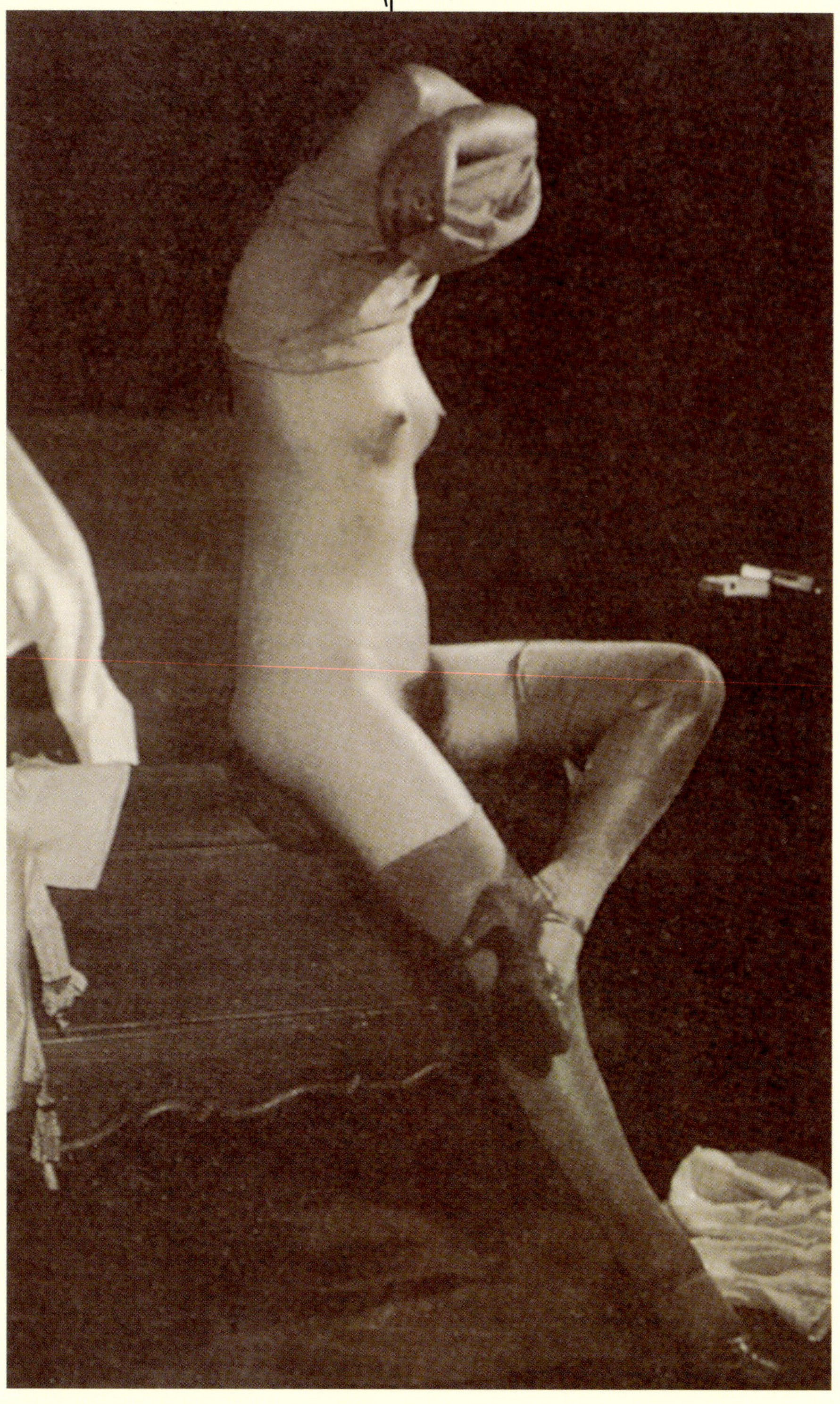

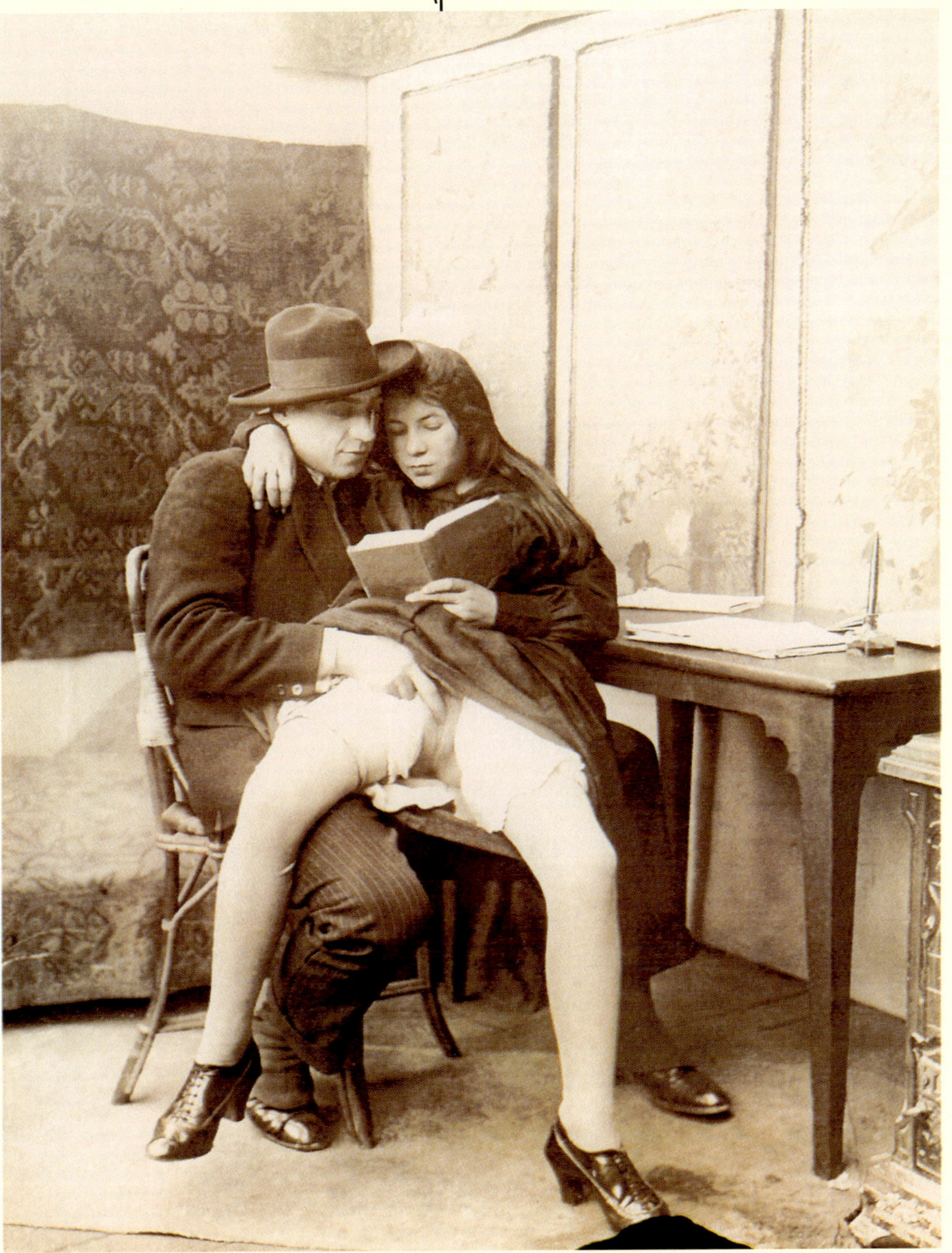

Preceding Pages:
2. Rojan, Voyeurs, around 1930.

3. Photo of a young Parisian girl, around 1900.
4. Photo, Paris, around 1900.

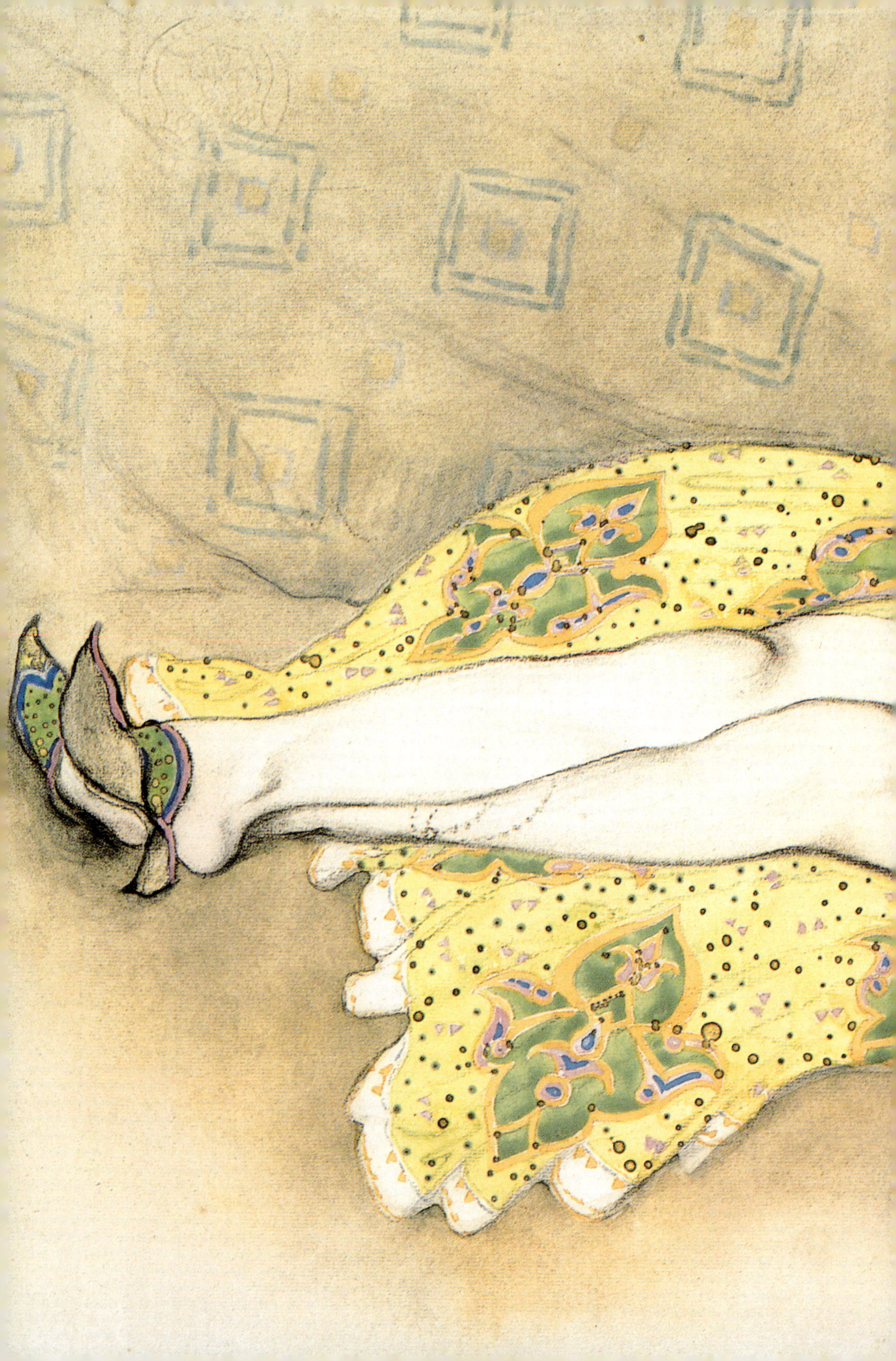

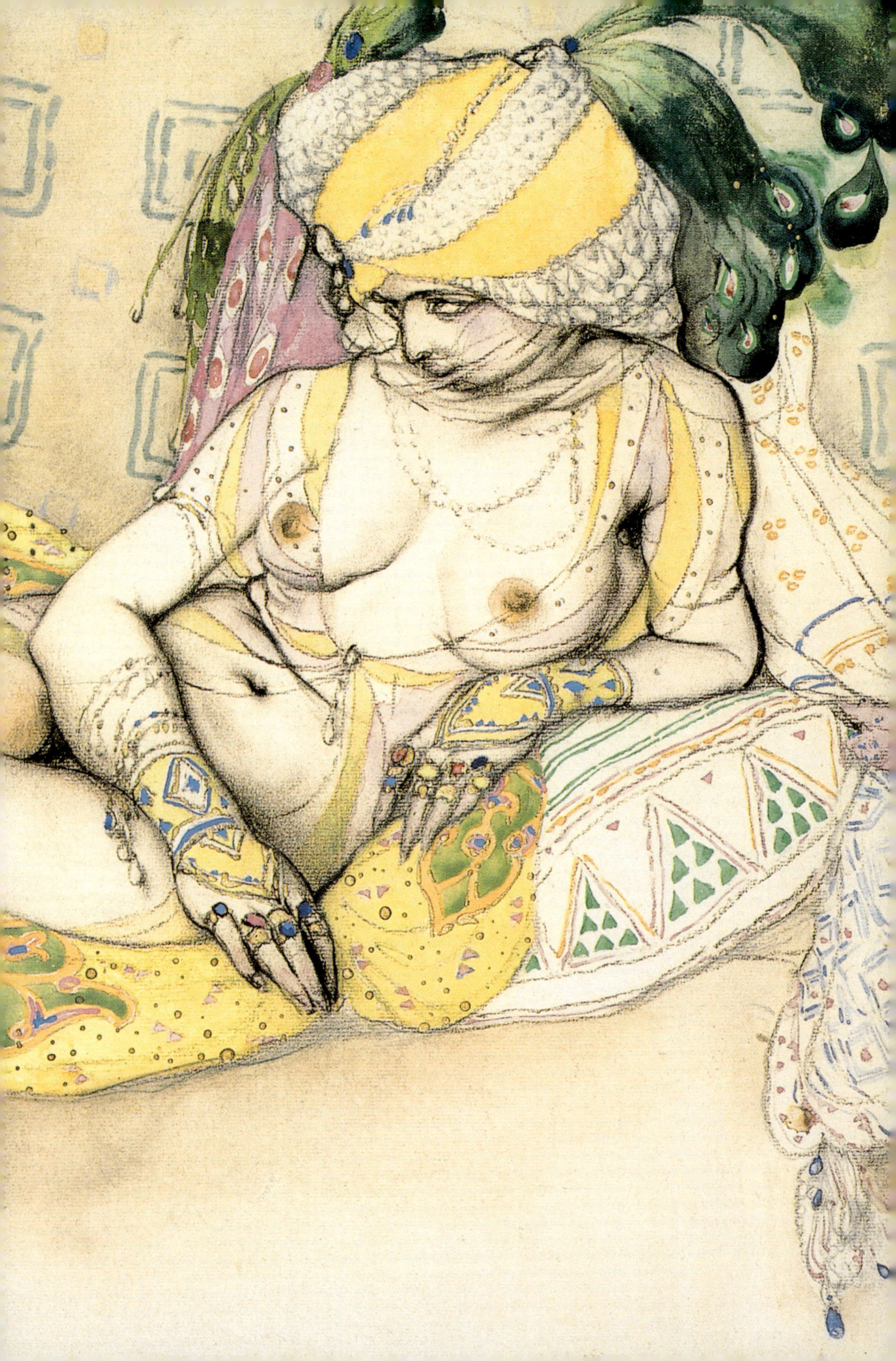

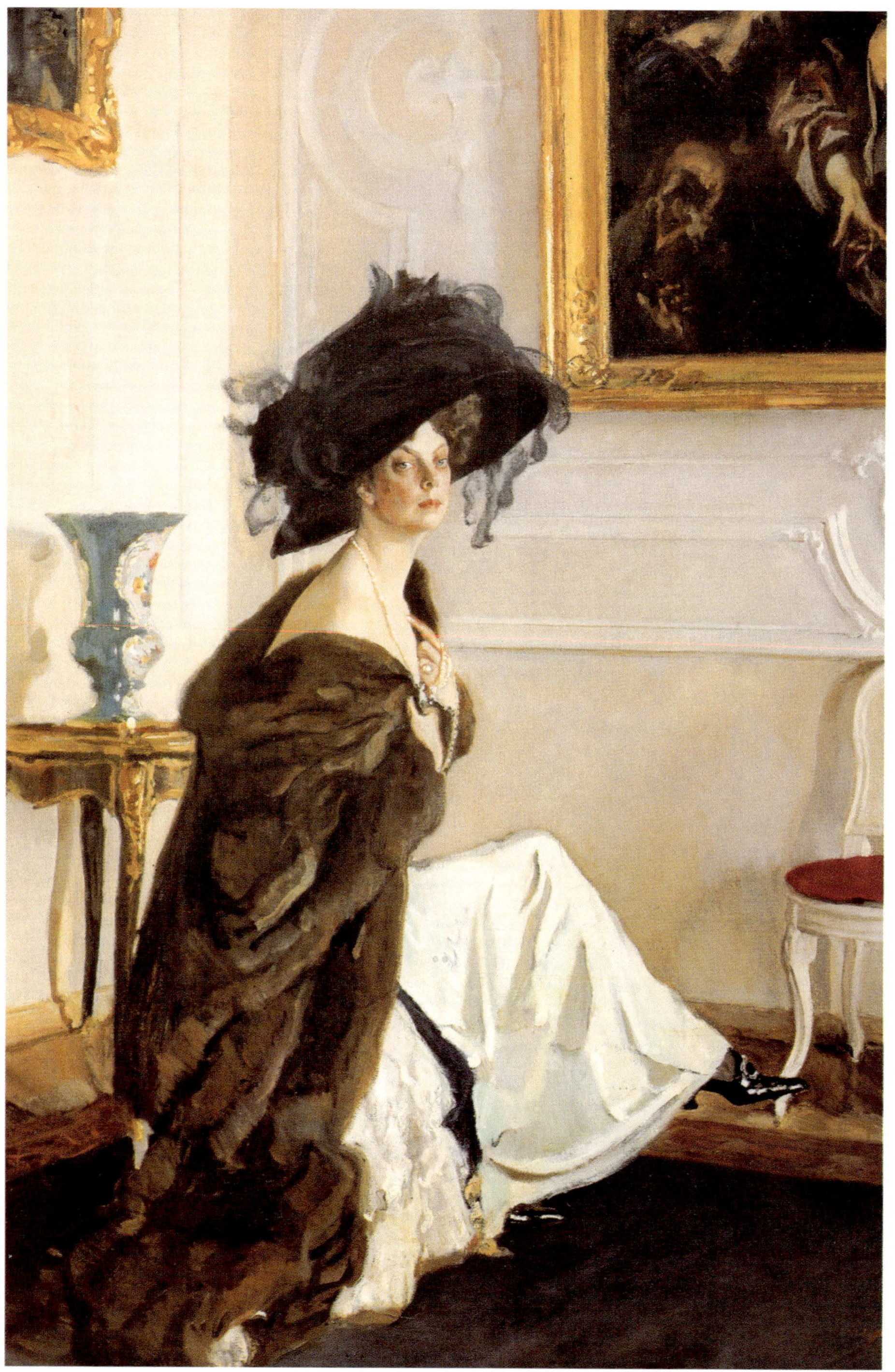

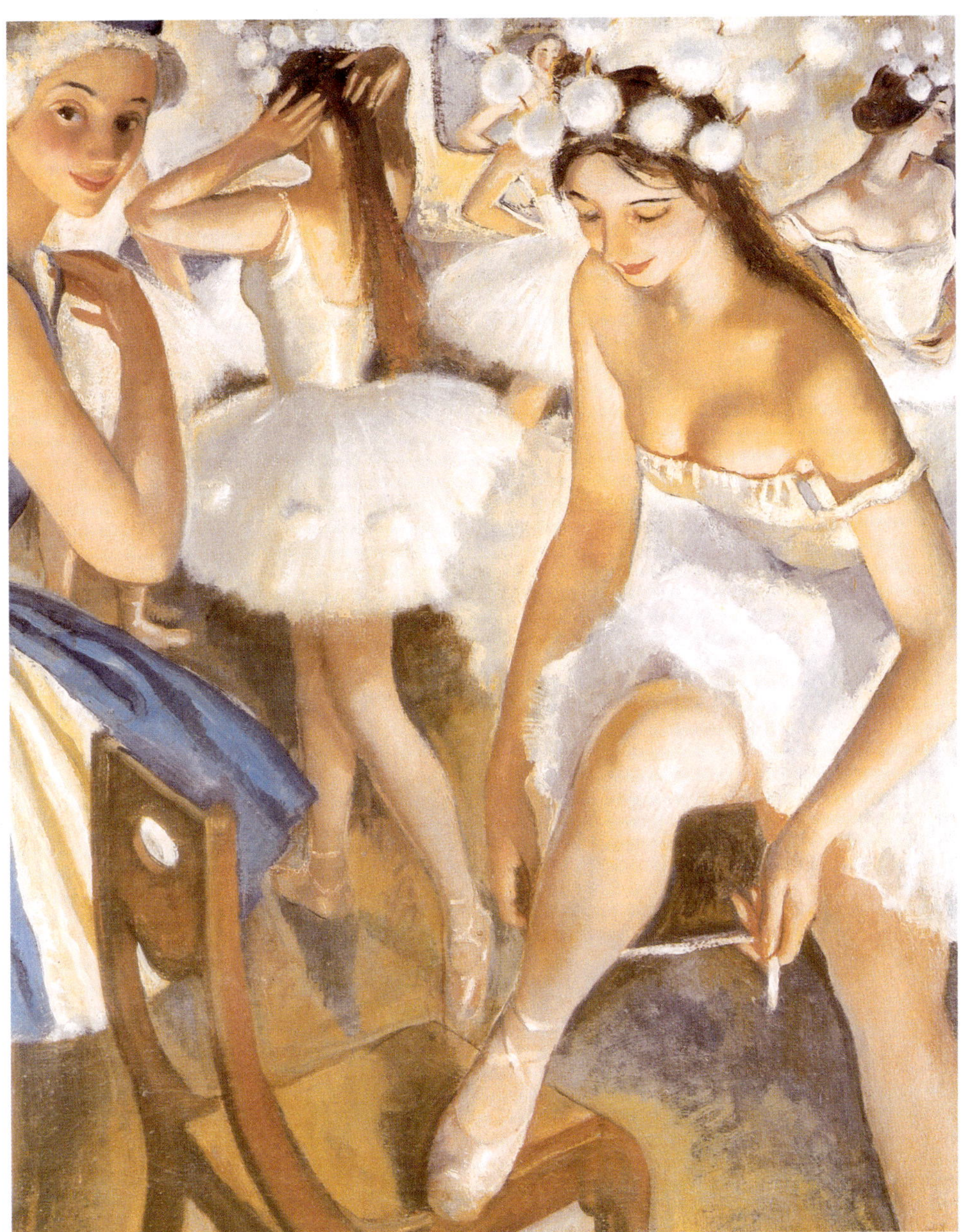

Preceding Pages:
5. Léon Bakst, La Sultane Jaune, 1916.
6. Valentin Serov, Portrait of the Princess Olga Orlova, 1911.

7. Zinaïda Serebriakova, Dancer's Dressing-room: Snow Crystals, 1923.

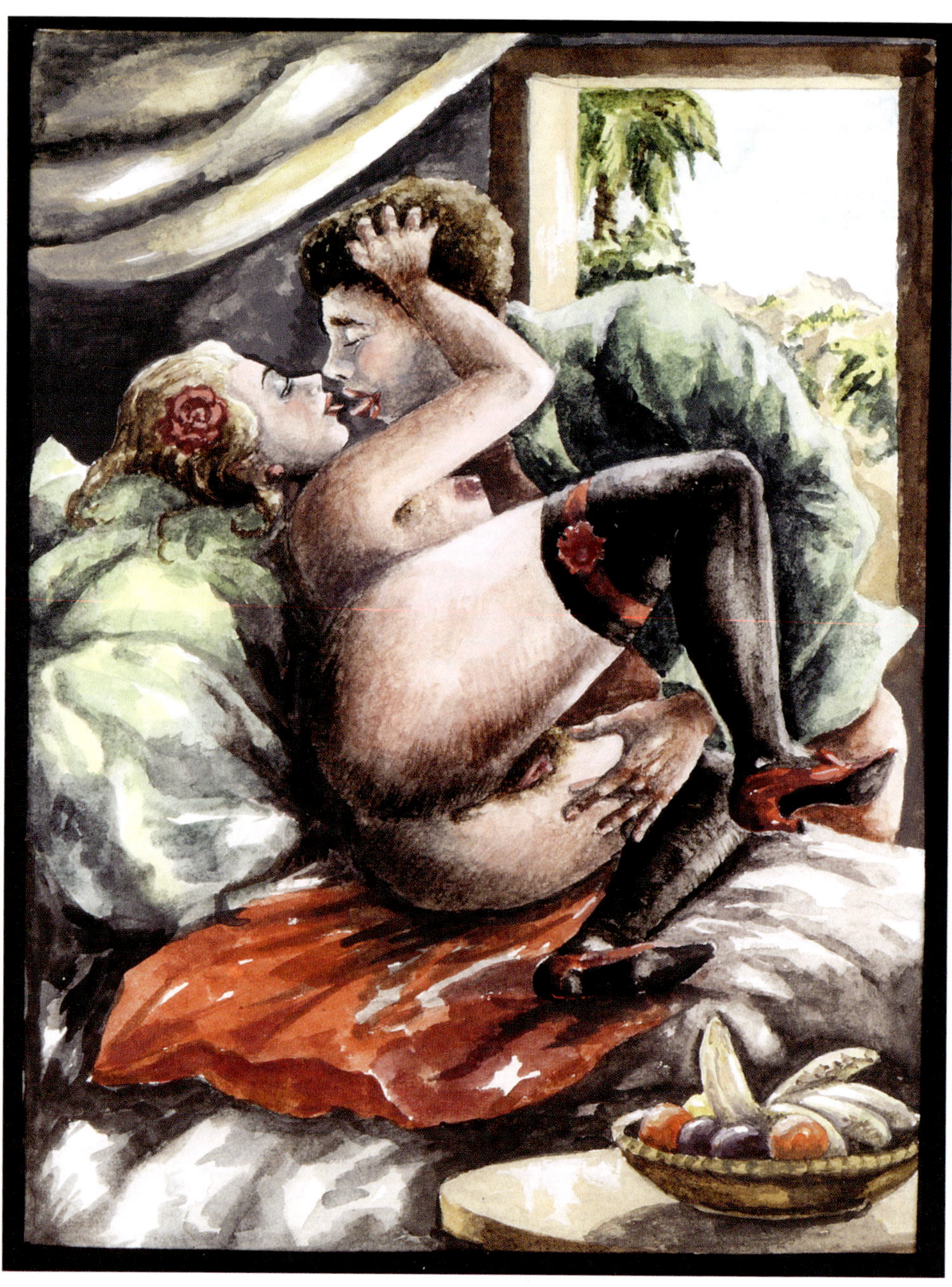

8. De Monceau, watercolour, around 1940.

However, there are forms where the sexual partner disappears completely behind the symbol – sometimes to the extent that the symbol is stripped of its symbolic character and becomes the sexual trigger and stimulus itself.

This is where parts of clothing, especially shoes, stockings, handkerchiefs, and underwear play a significant role. Cases are known in classical literature where handkerchiefs, clothing, money purses, and braids are snatched from their owners through violence and trickery to satisfy a sexual motive, while orgasm occurs in part during the act of purloining, in part through masturbation when viewing or handling the fetish.

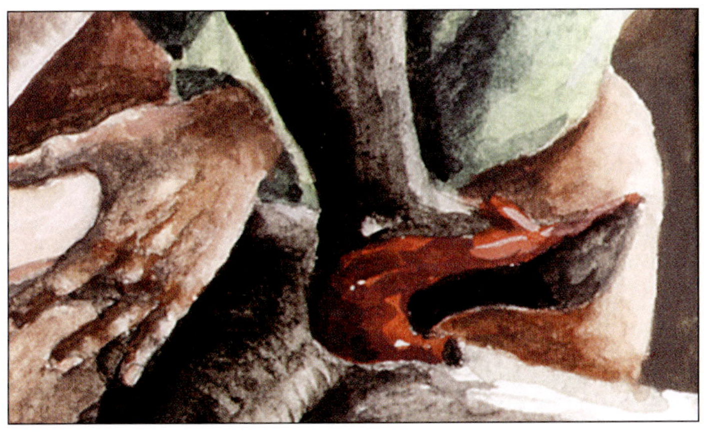

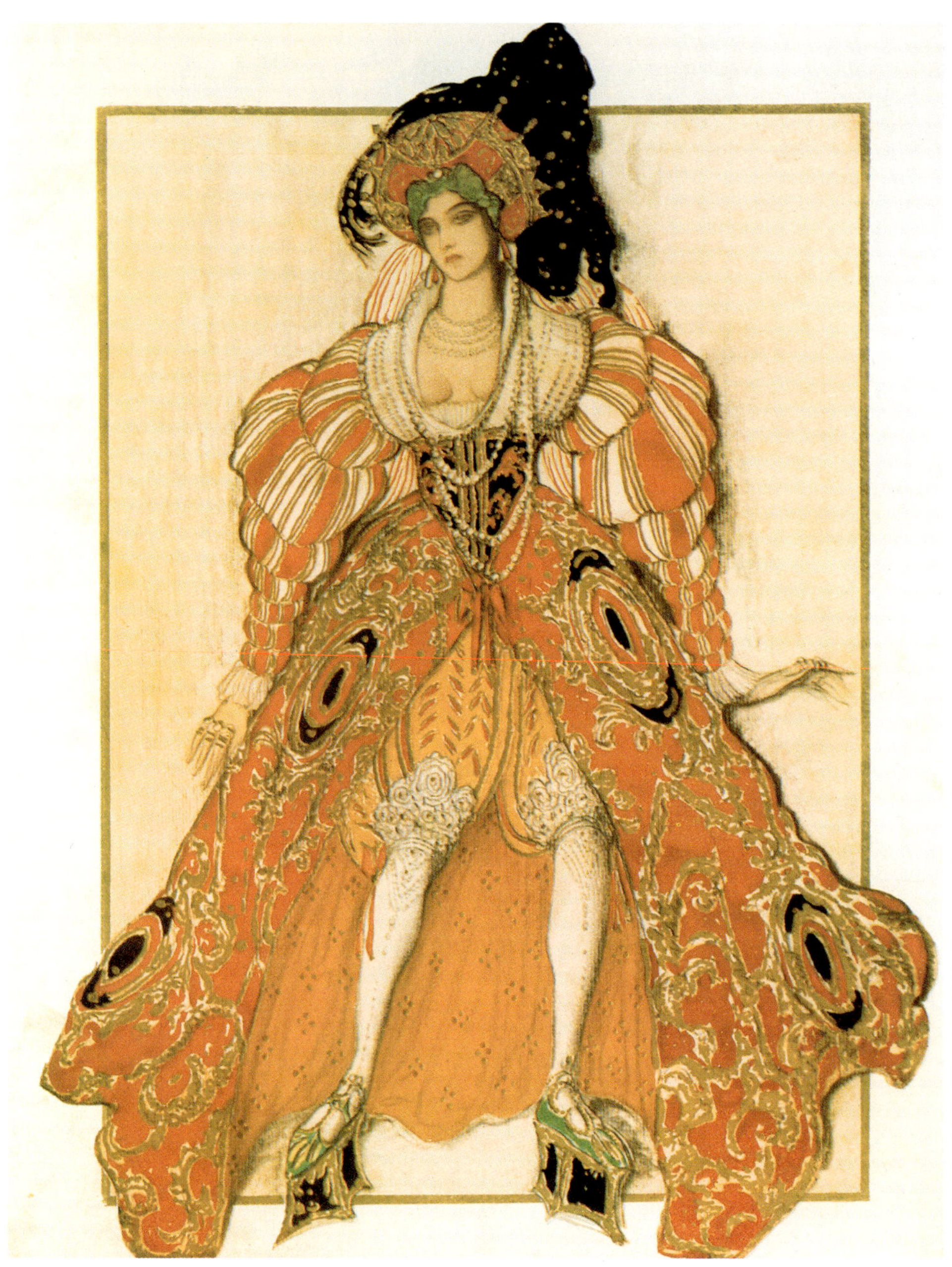

9. Léon Bakst, costume design for Potiphar's wife, La Légende de Joseph, 1914.
10. Egon Schiele, The Green Stocking, 1914.

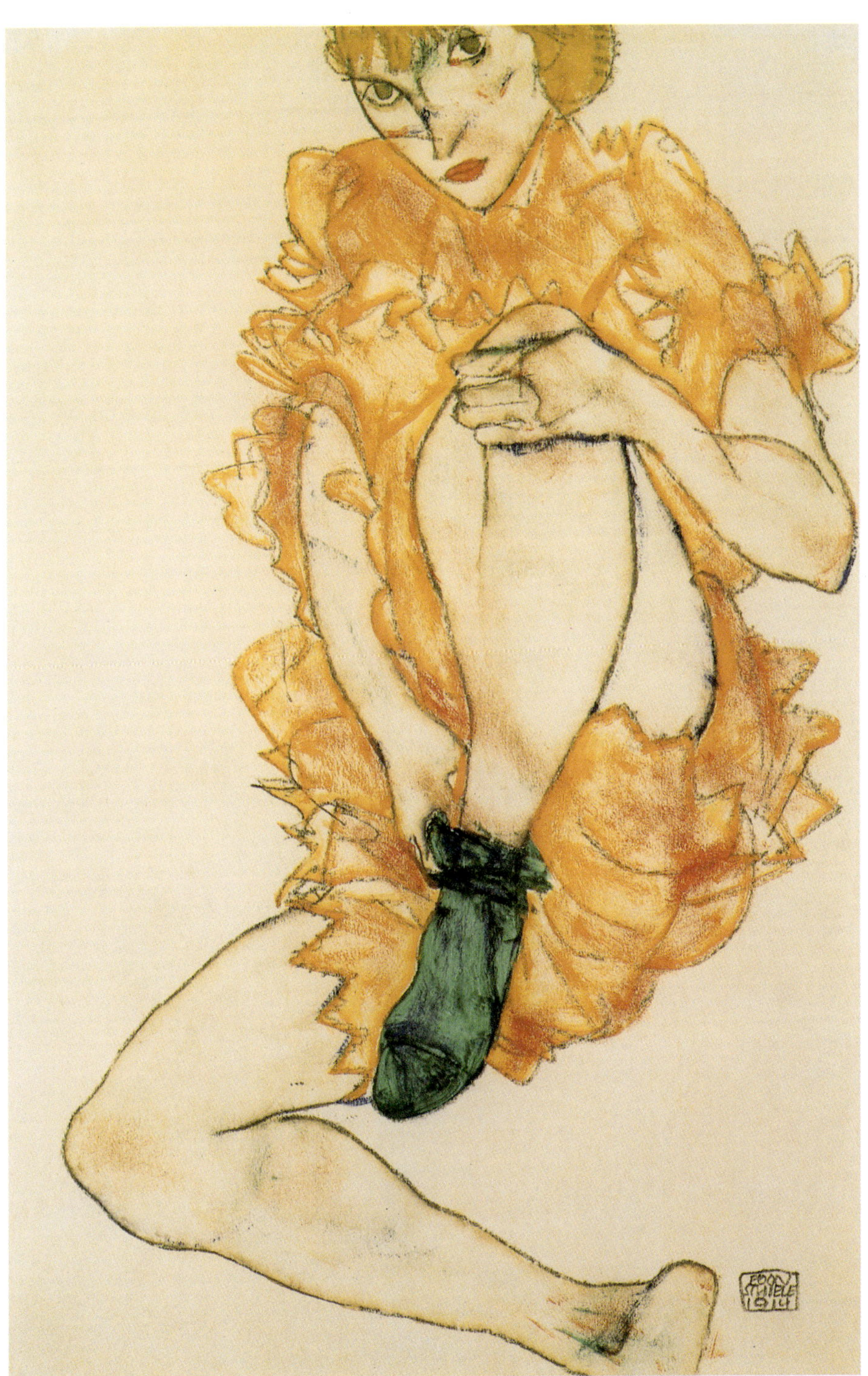

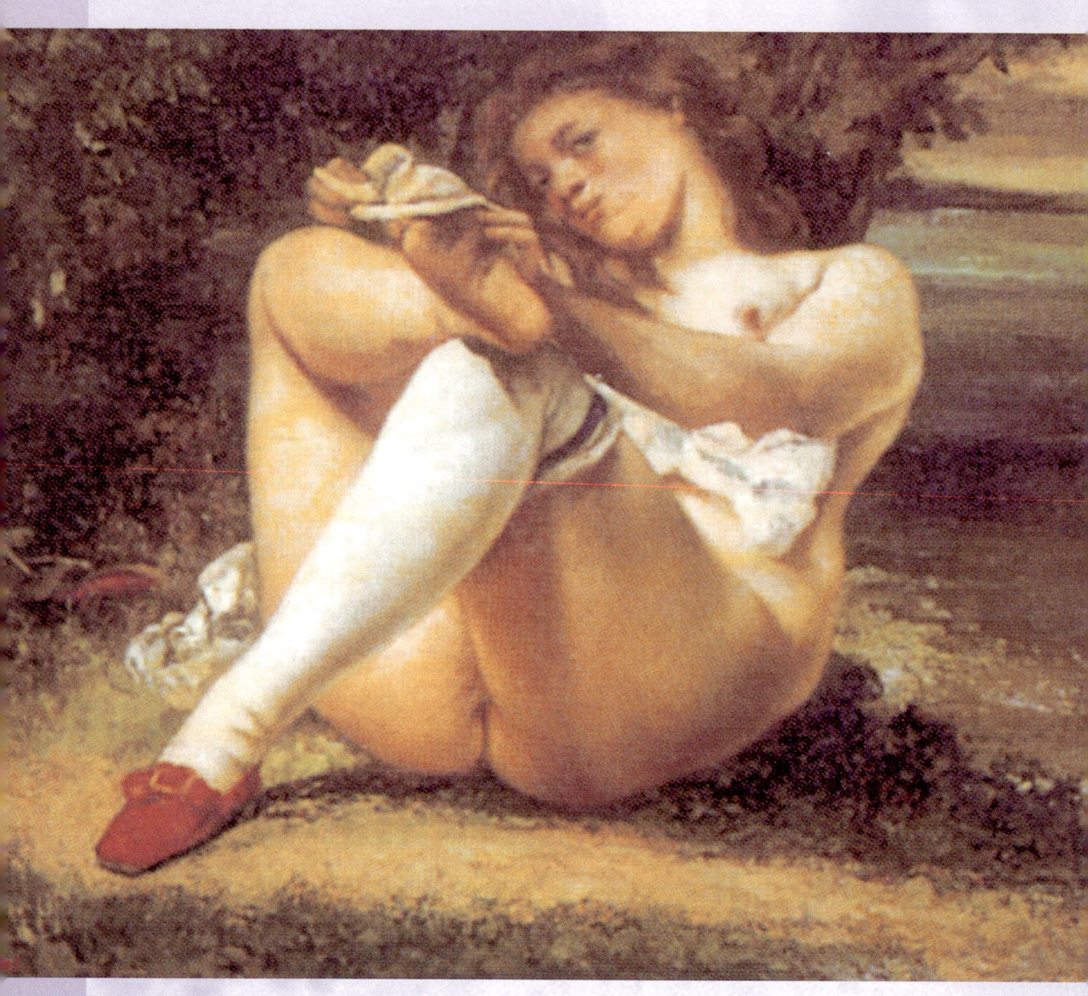

11. Gustave Courbet, Woman in White Stockings, 1861.

*A*ll of these objects are charged with magical powers similar to the relics as known by the church and the amulets of so-called "indigenous tribes." The term applied to the phenomenon of fetishism also has its roots in ethnology.

During the 15th and 16th century, when the Portuguese in West Africa noticed the reverence and veneration with which the local natives treated such objects as stones, sticks, and idols, they compared these objects with amulets or talismans and called them "feiticio" [Italian: "fetisso"] or "magic," a word which is derived from the Latin "factitius" [of magic power].

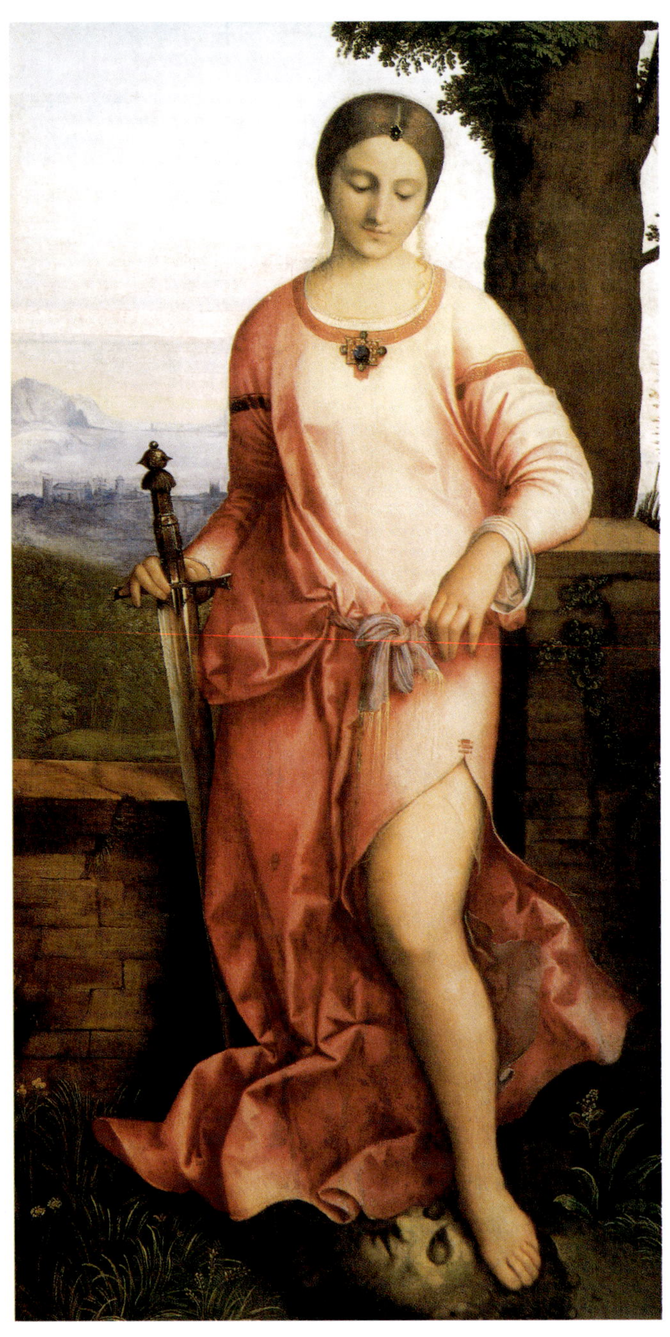

12. Giorgione, Judith, around 1500.

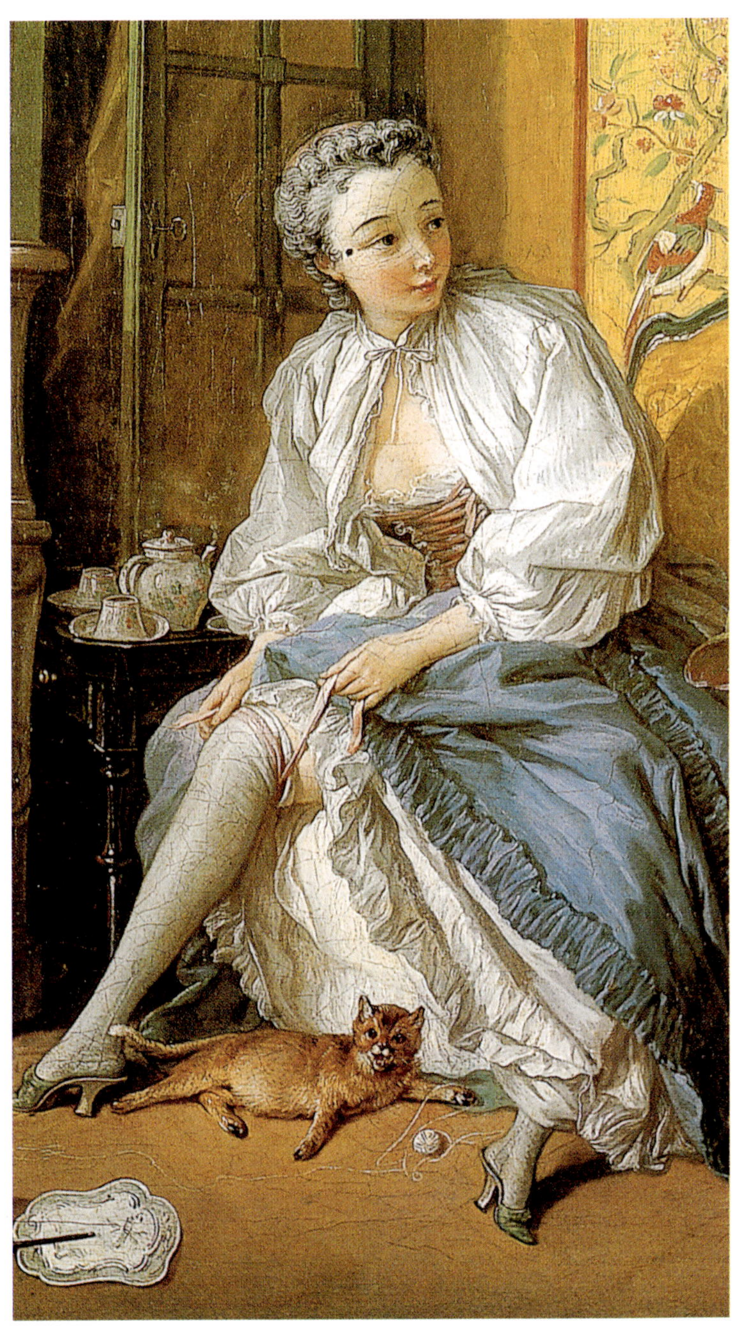

13. François Boucher, La Toilette (detail), 1742.

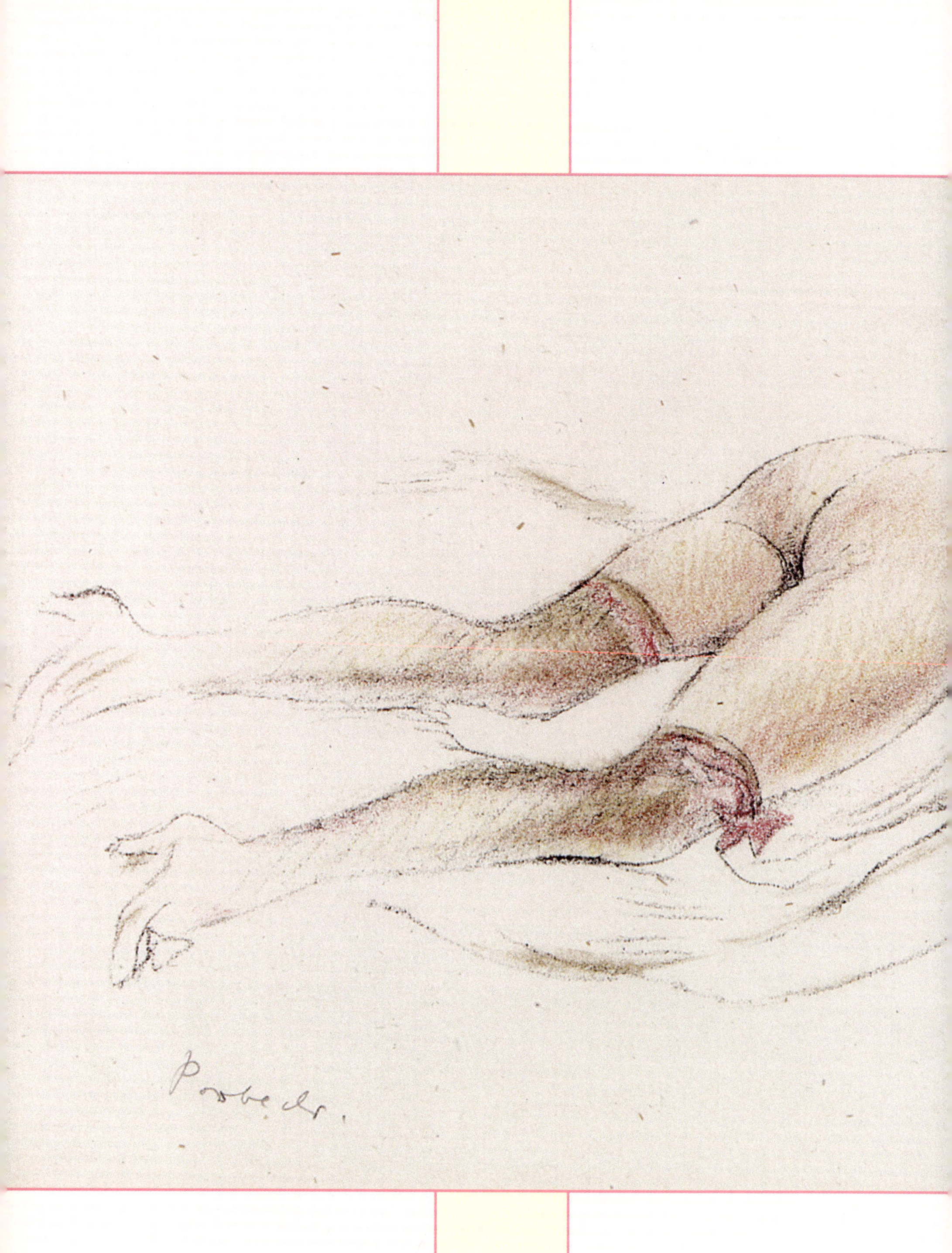

14. Otto Schoff, colour lithograph, around 1930.

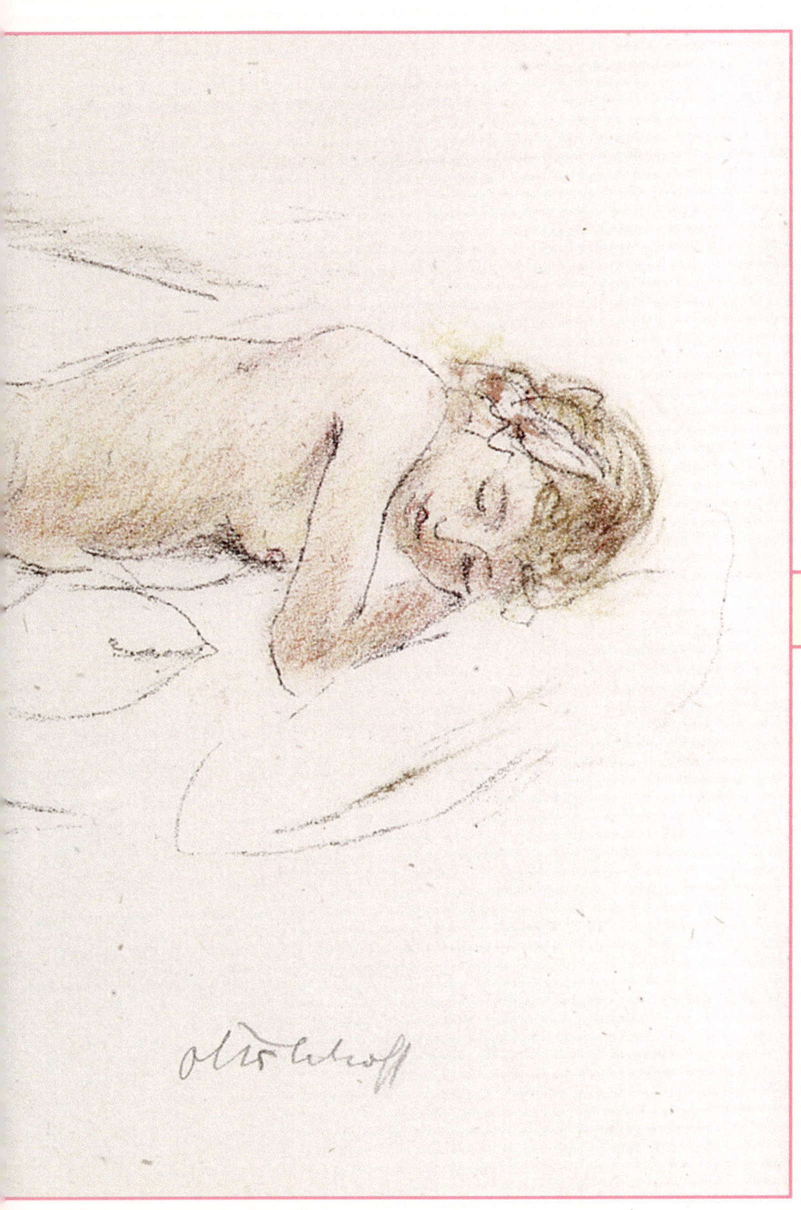

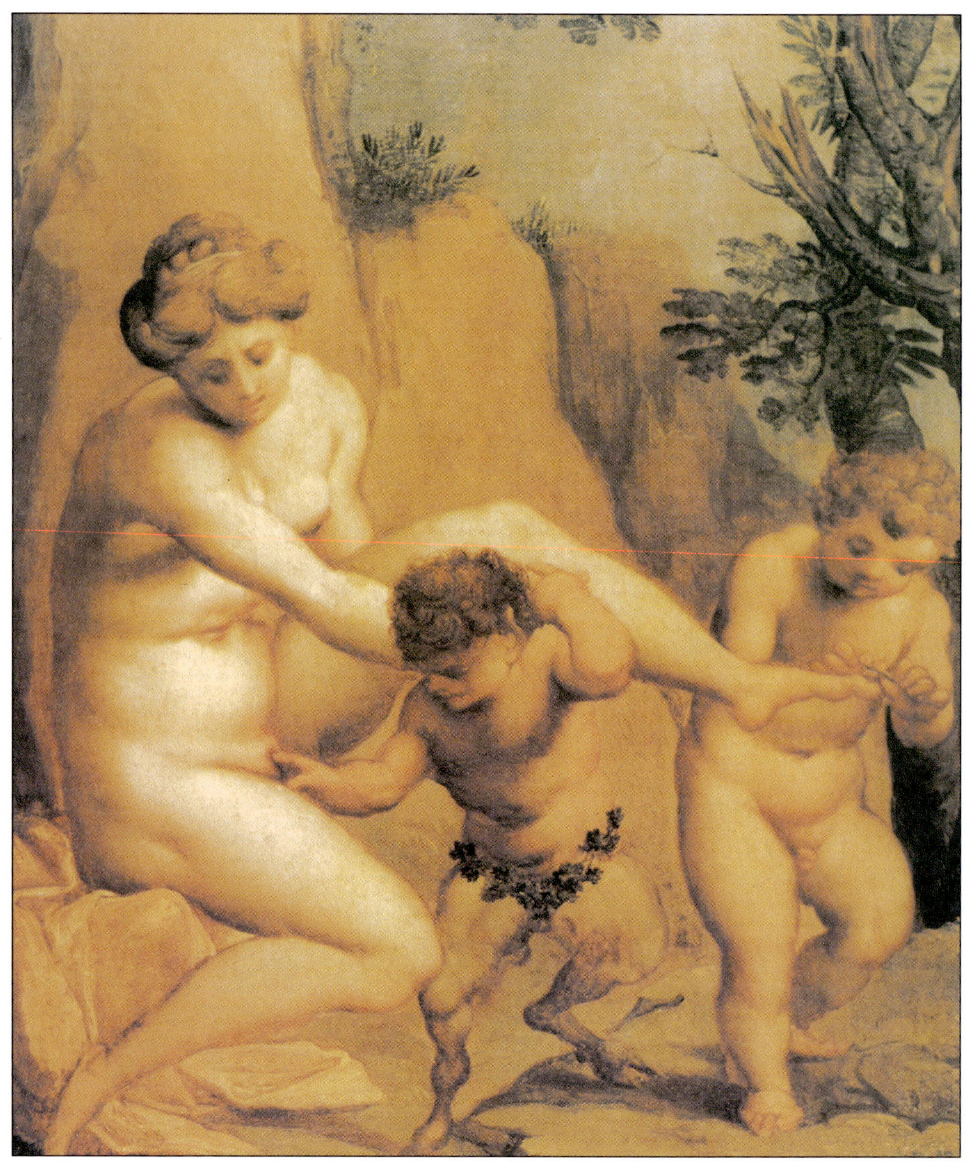

15. Anonymous, Venus, Goddess of Love, 17th century.
16. Anonymous design dating from the 1950s, Germany.

This magical thinking, which also penetrated the cults of Christian religion, corresponds with a deep, human need. Those who are aware of the close relationship between religious and erotic sensations and feelings understand that fetishistic imagery also occurs frequently in love. The Frenchman A. Binet was the first to describe sexual fetishism in his 1877 article "Du fétichisme dans l`amour."

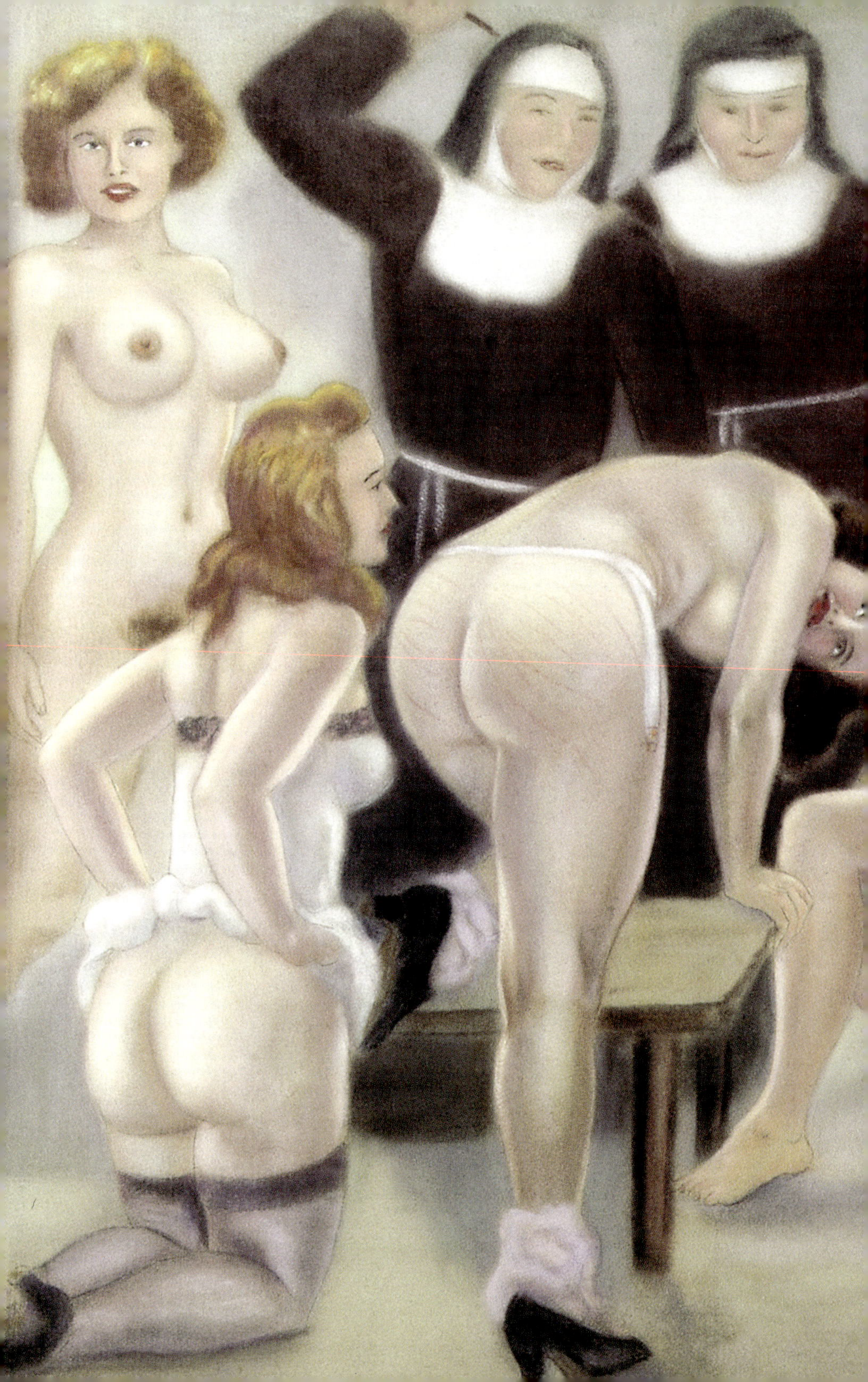

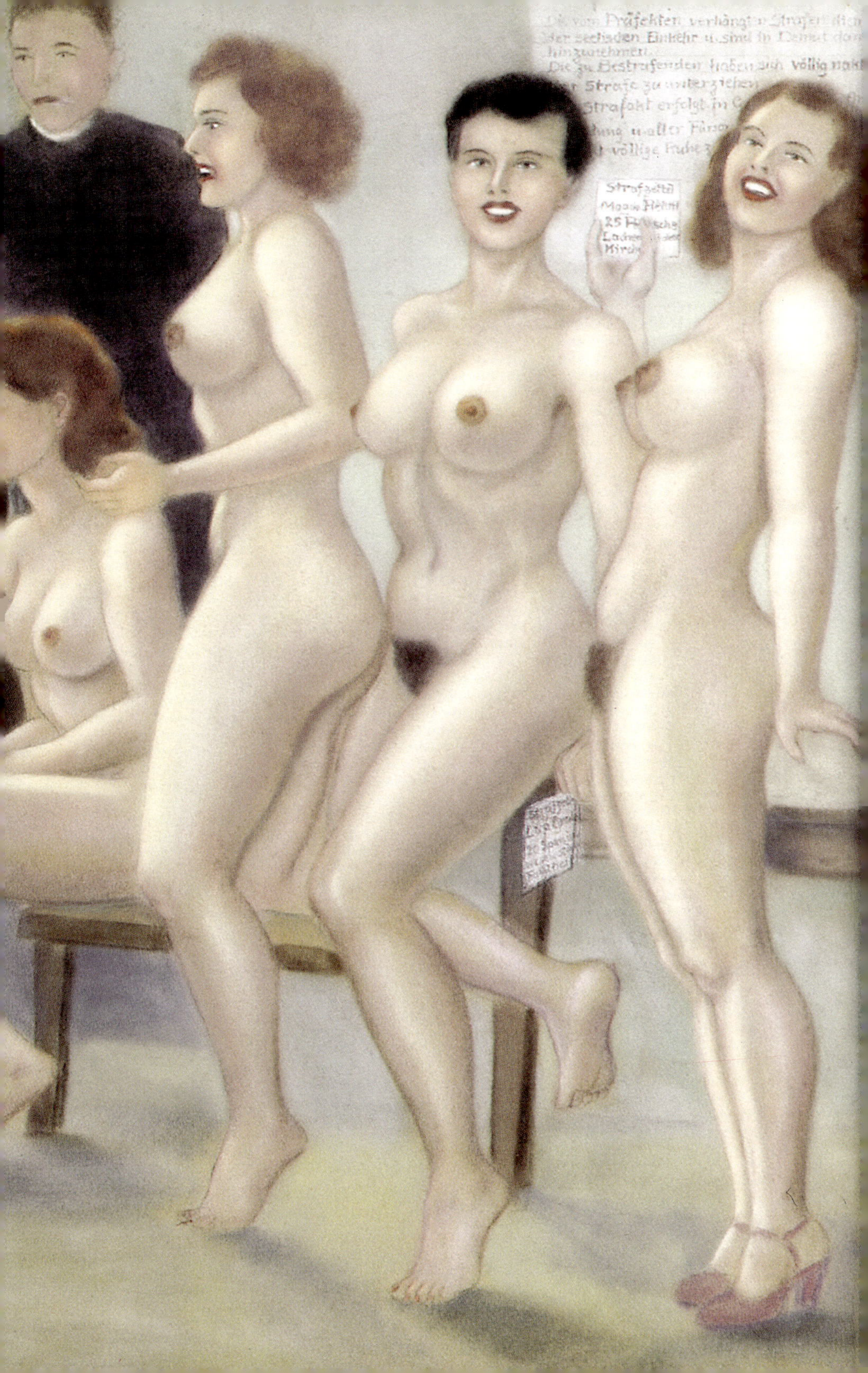
Die vom Präfekten verhängten Strafen sind
der seeligen Einkehr u. sind in Demut dem
hinzuziehen.
Die zu Bestrafenden haben sich völlig nackt
der Strafe zu unterziehen
Strafakt erfolgt in G
ung u aller Fürso
völlige Ruhe

Strafzettel
Maria Rohm
25 Rutsche
Lachen in der
Kirche

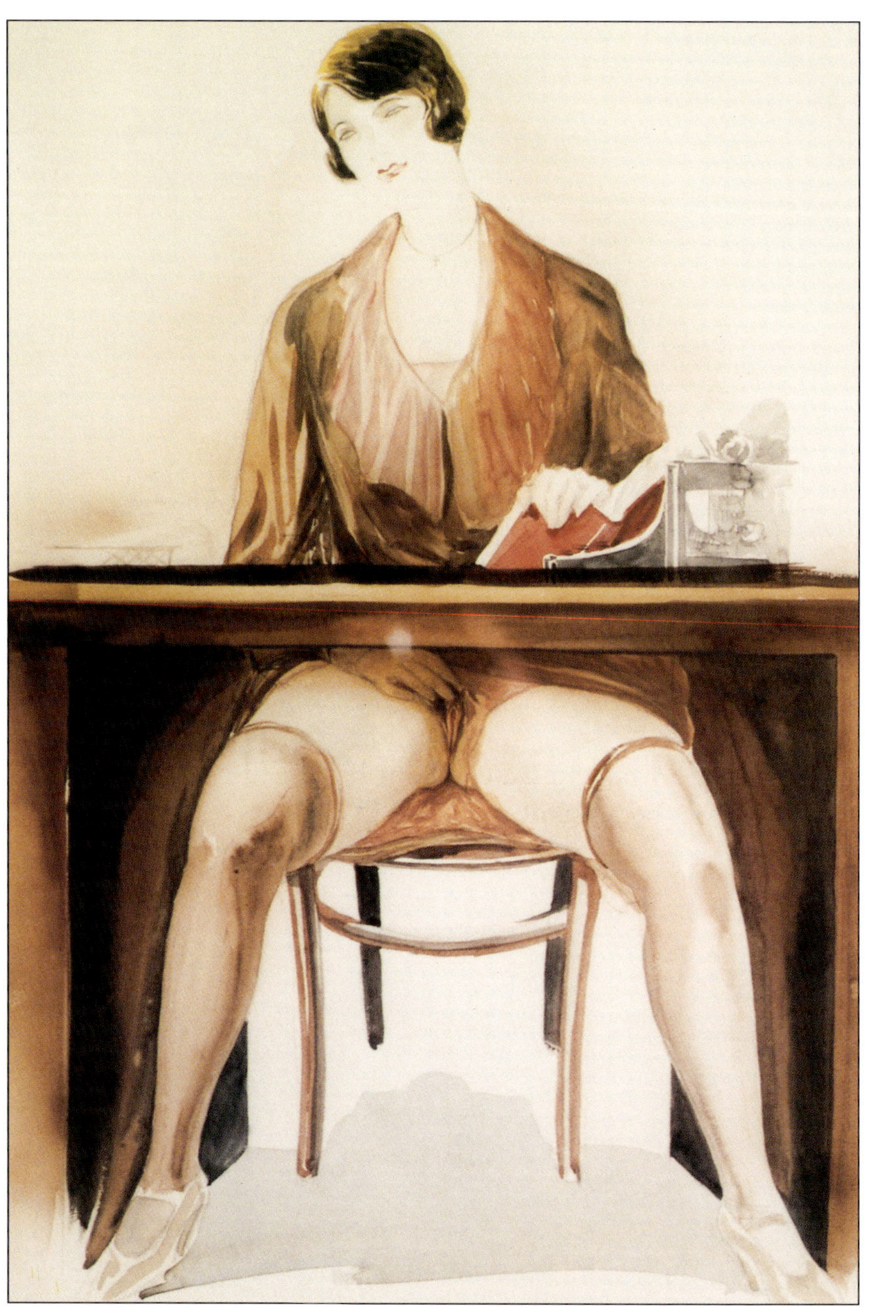

The few mentioned examples of fetish-istic objects already illustrate how much the fetishes themselves depend on current fashions. The old braids have been cut off a long time ago and a paper Kleenex will hardly be an object feverishly desired by a lover. The shoe and foot fetish was influenced by fashion as well. When women still wore long skirts with their feet every so often accidentally peeking out from underneath, it was literally a "fiendish joy" to steal a glance of leg and shoe. When calves were still hidden from view, never mind the knees, the calf fetishists were happy about bad weather: This gave them the opportunity to follow women for long stretches in the hopes that the ladies might be forced to lift their skirts because of the puddles and thus expose their calves to the greedy looks of their pursuers.

Concealment steered the imagination towards calves, feet, and footwear, and promoted the fetishistic preference for these body parts and their clothing.

17. Rojan, watercolour, 1925.

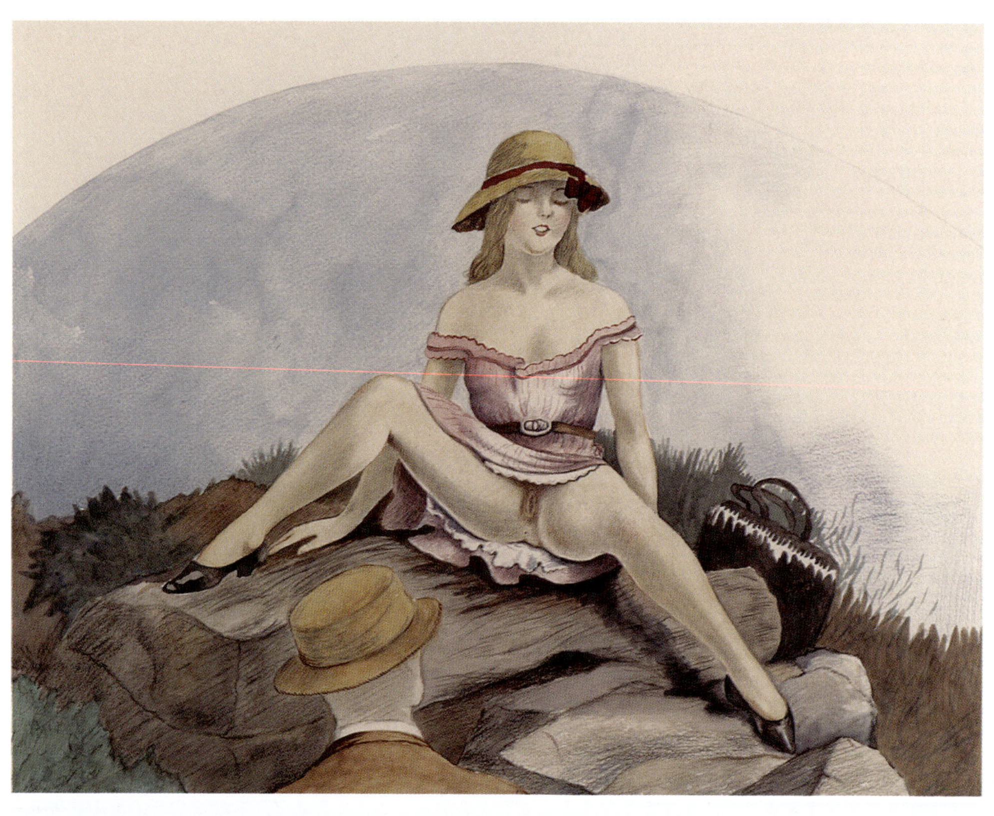

18. Rojan, Voyeurs, around 1930.

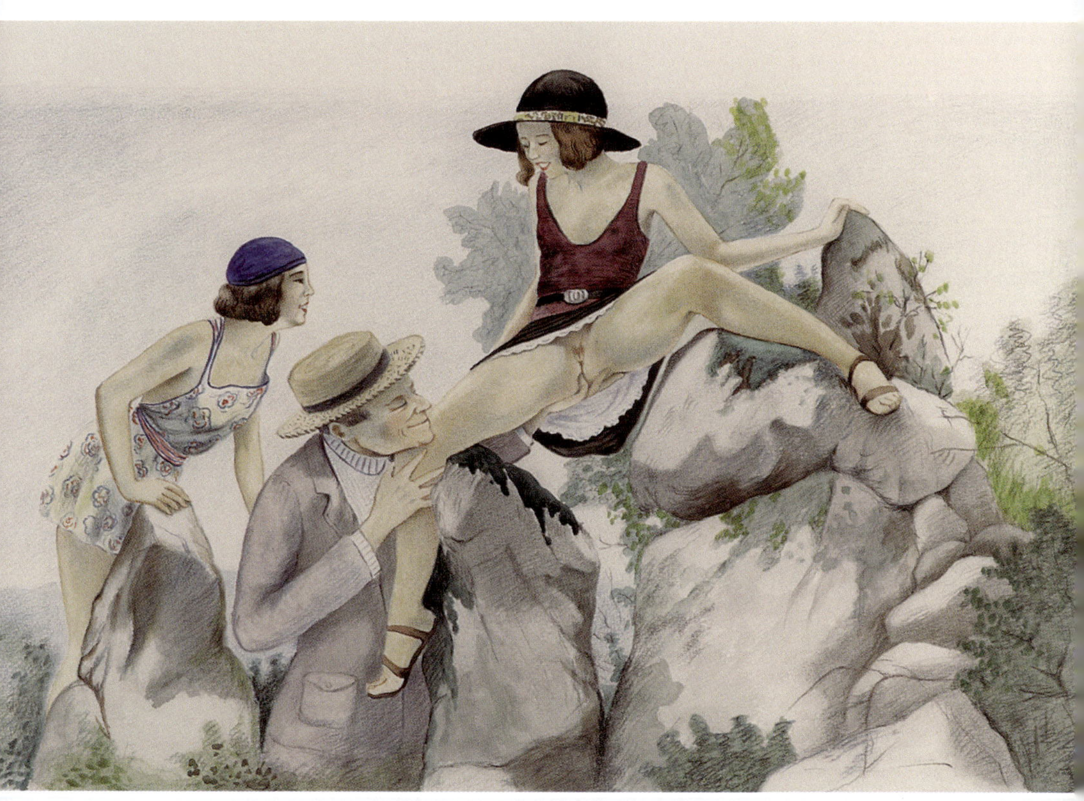

19. Rojan, Voyeurs, around 1930.

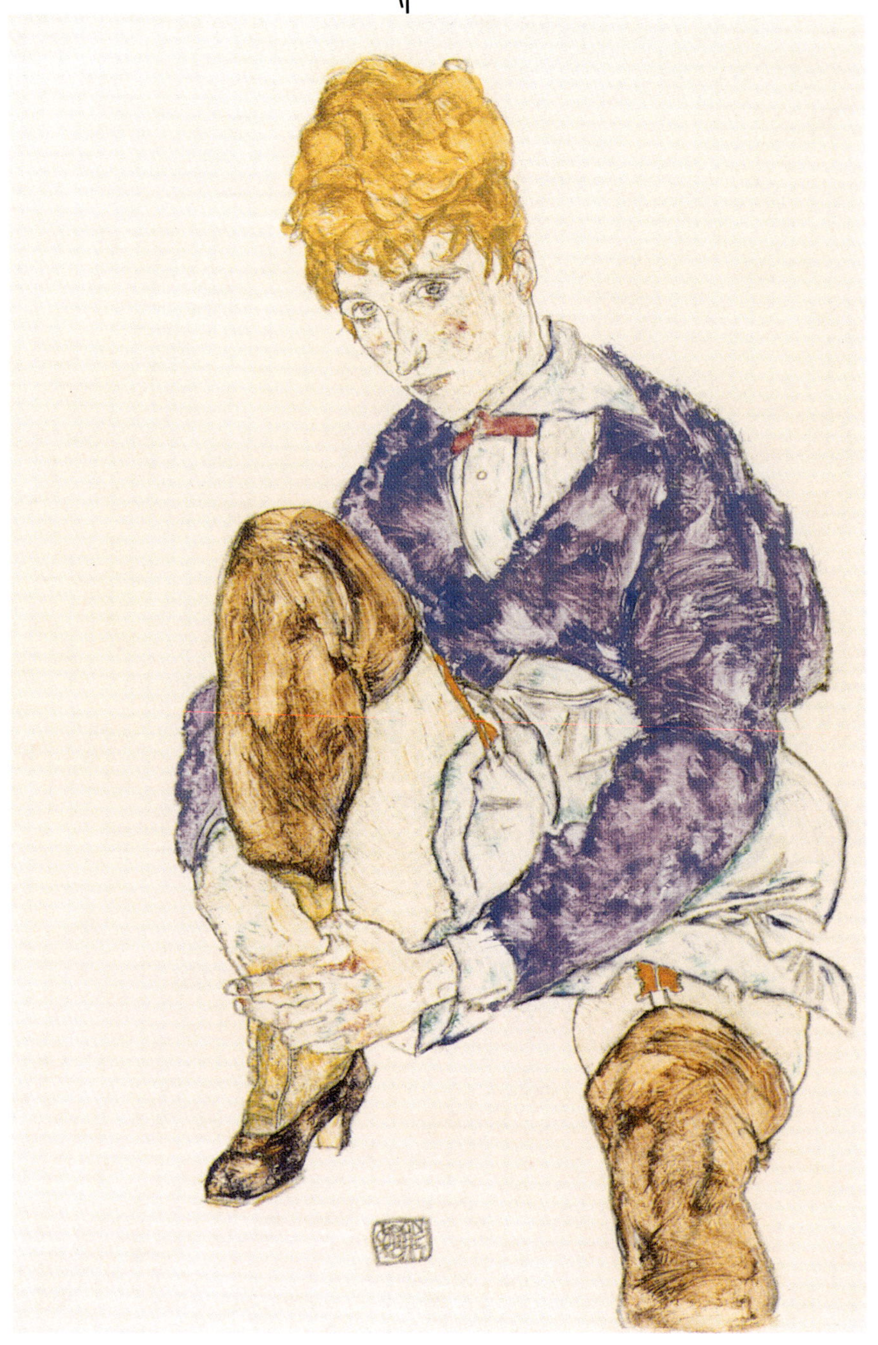

20. Egon Schiele, Portrait of the Artist's Wife Holding Her Right Leg, 1917.

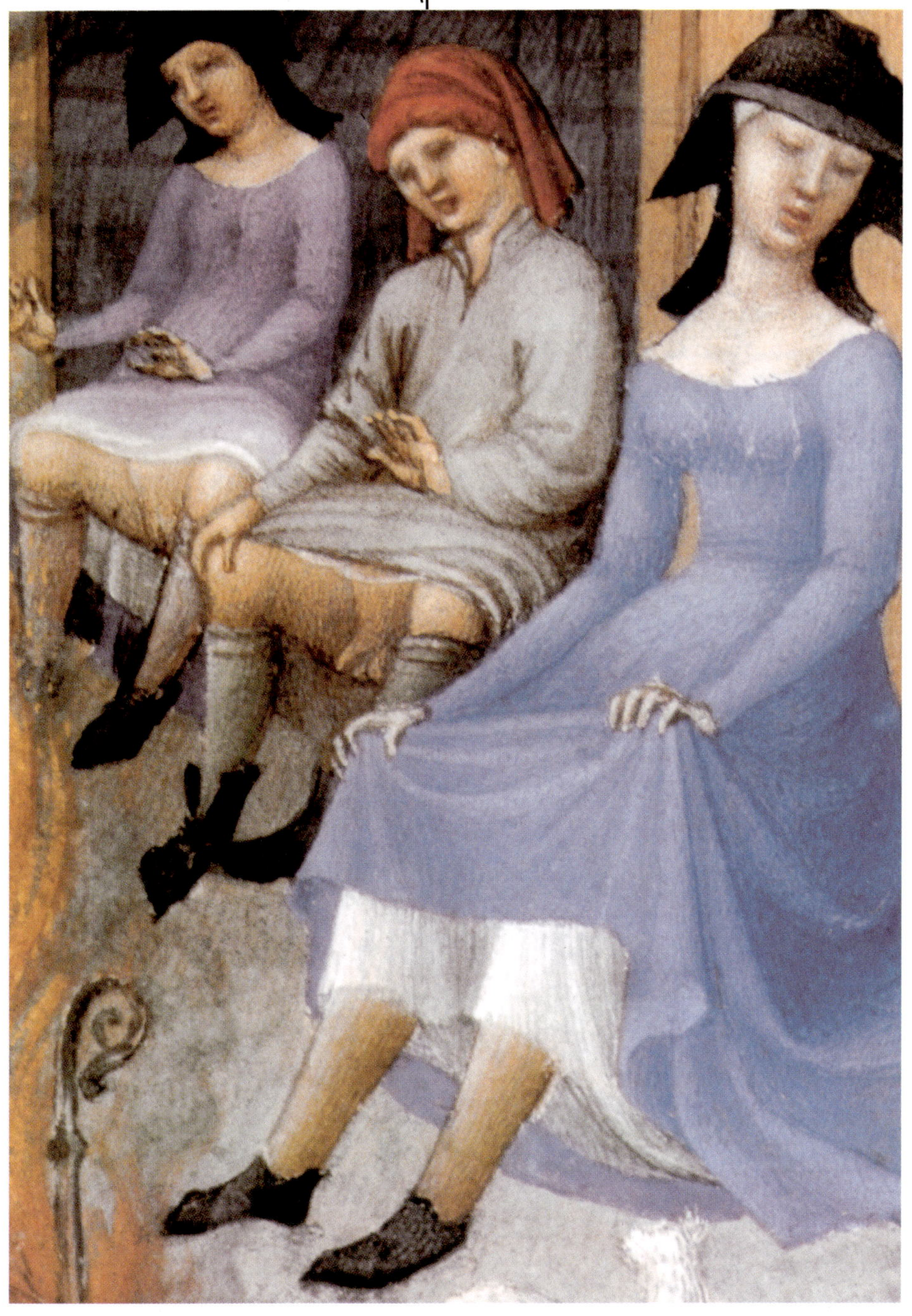

21. Rosarium Philosophorum, Les Très Riches Heures du Duc du Berry, 1556.

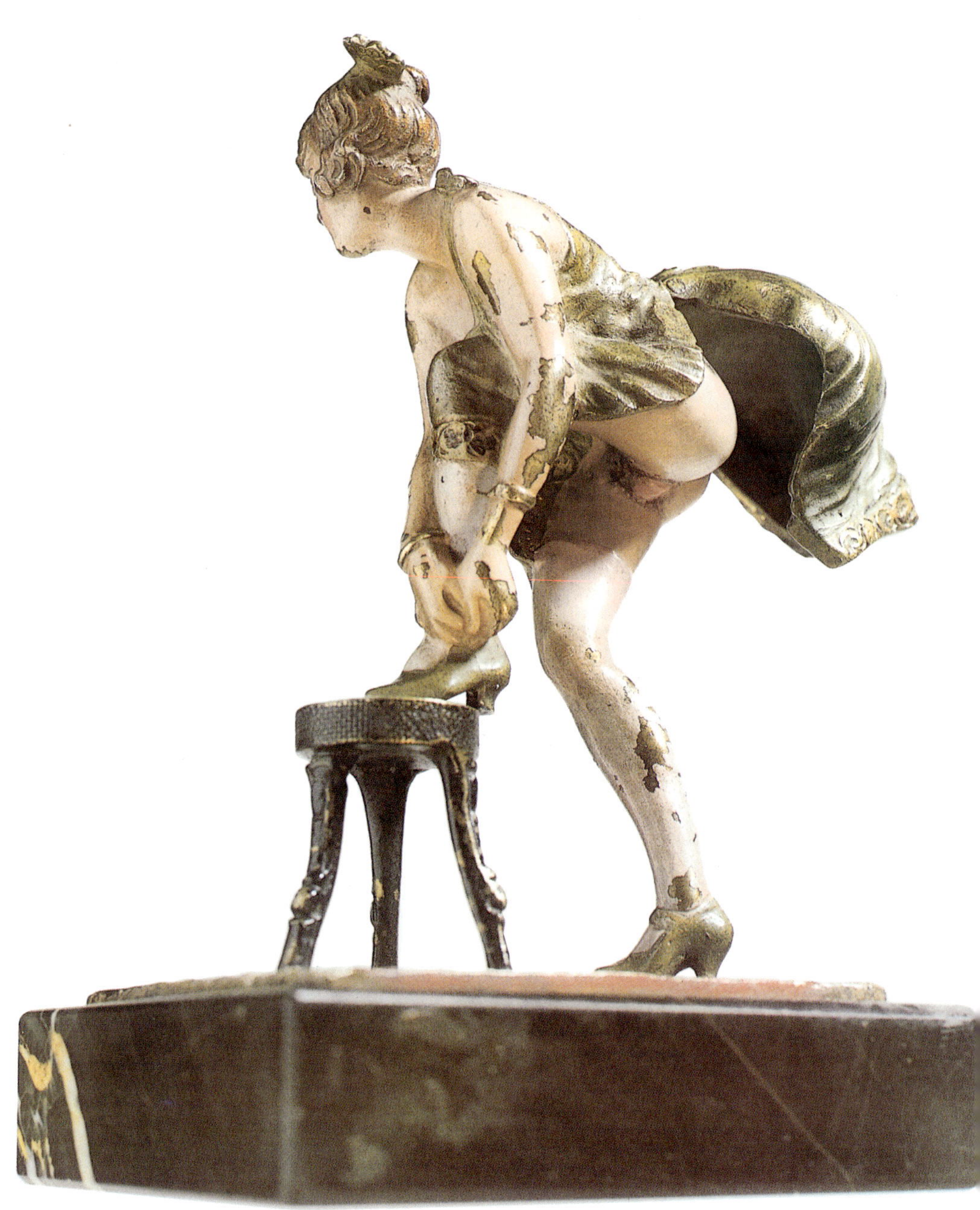

22. Cold-painted bronze dating from the end of the 19th century.

There were shoe fetishists who aroused themselves with the shoes and boots that used to be placed outside the doors of hotel rooms for cleaning. Hirschfeld describes the case of a man who engaged in masturbation when he looked at a pair of large men's boots, preferably a soldier's boots with spurs, next to delicate women's shoes that were placed outside the door; during the cover of night, he would sneak over to where the shoes were to caress, smell, and kiss them.

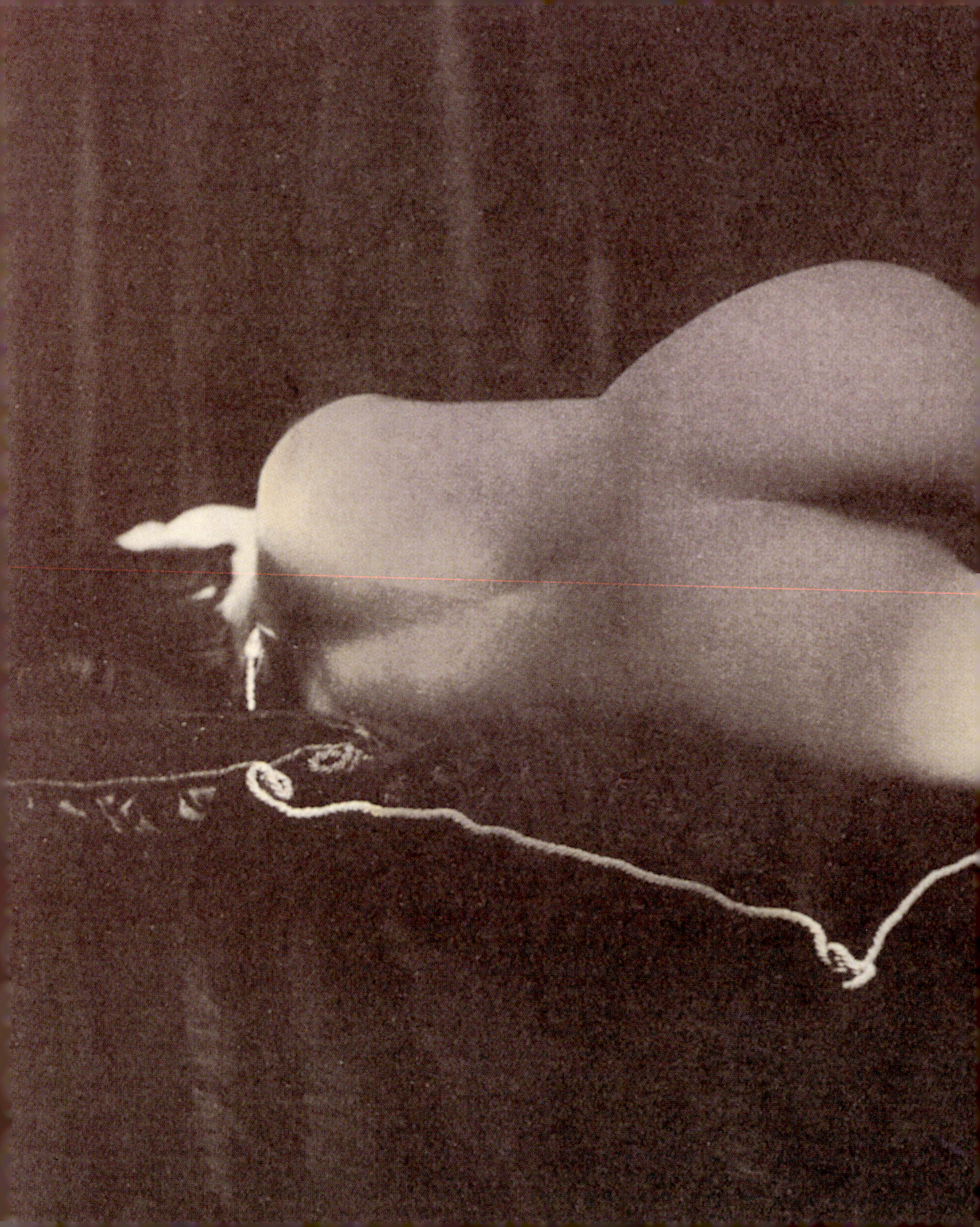

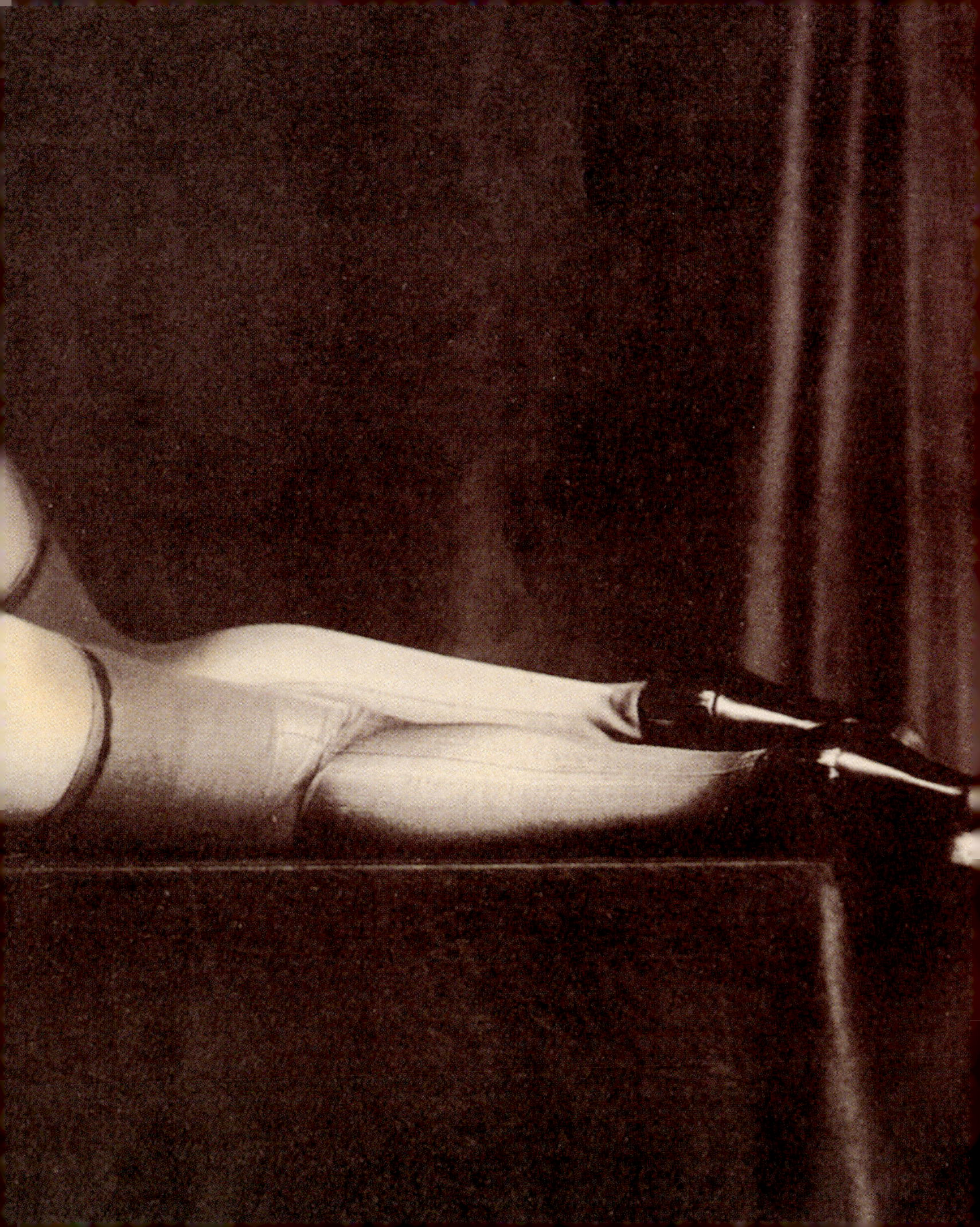

An expressive example of how foot and shoe can be nothing more than a fetishistic object is provided by the French writer Rétif de la Bretonne (1734 – 1806). He represents the type of a pure shoe fetish. When looking at women's shoes he used to quiver lustfully and blushed in front of them as if they were the girls themselves. He collected slippers and shoes of his lover, kissed and smelled them, and sometimes masturbated into them.

In his autobiographical novel Monsieur Nicolas, Rétif wrote the following about his shoe fetish:

Preceding Pages :
23. Photo, Paris, early years of the 20th century.
24. Orgiastic Dream, lithograph.

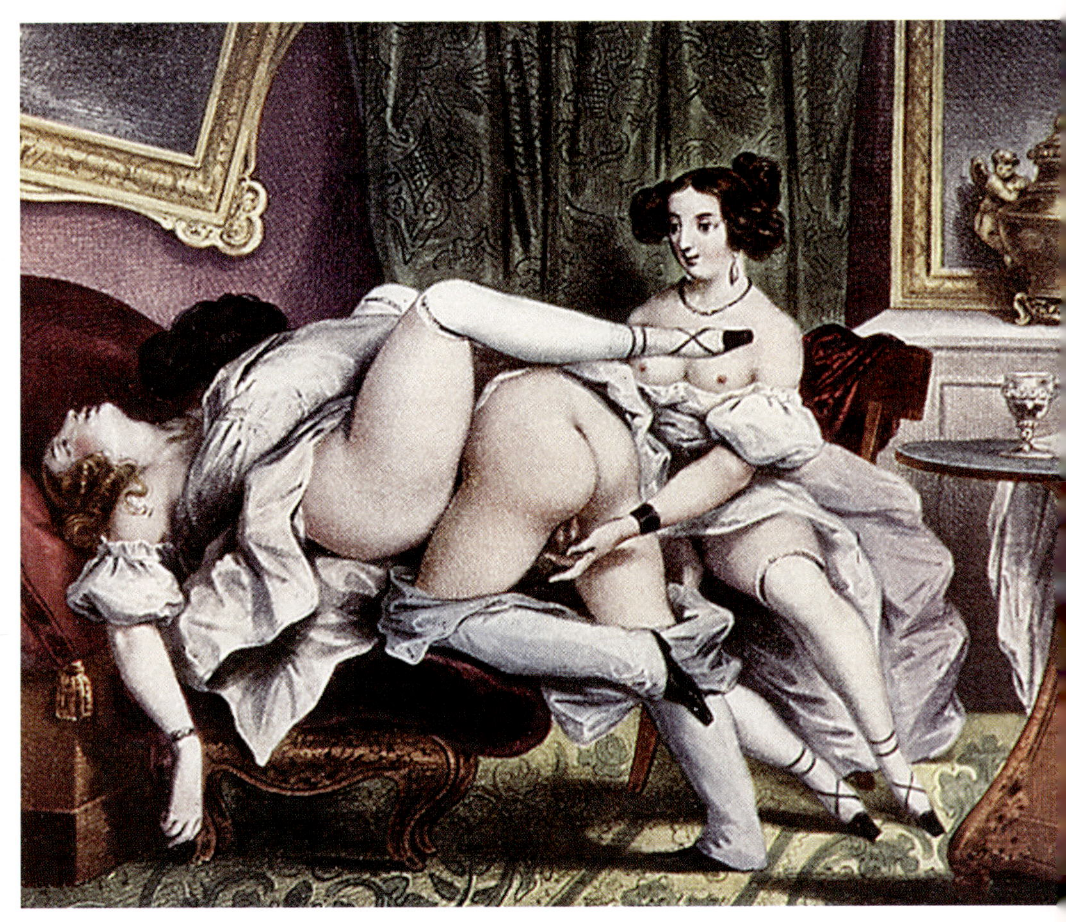

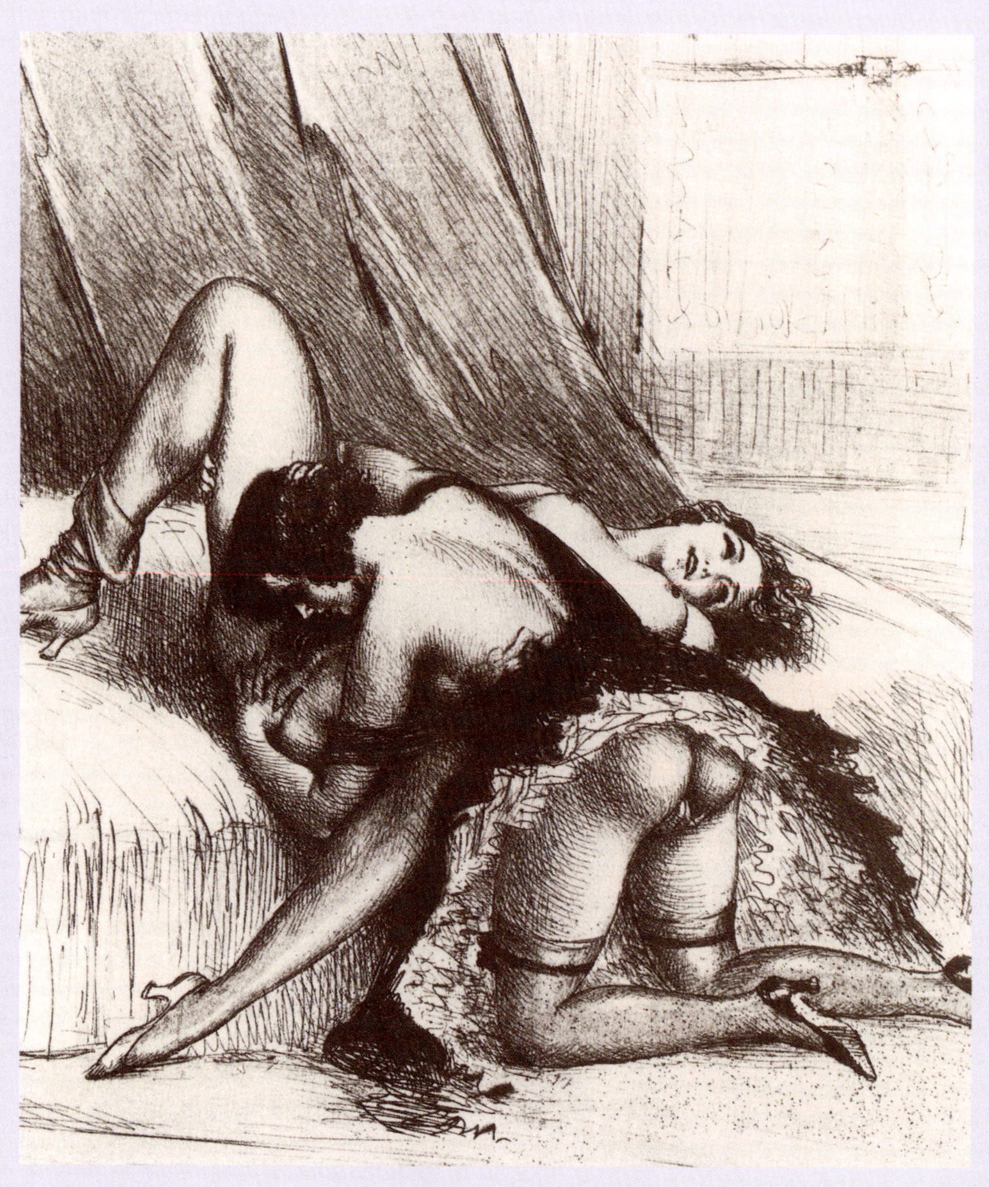

25. Anonymous French etching, 1910.

"Dragged away from the stormiest, completely adoring passion for Colette, I imagined seeing and feeling her in body and spirit by caressing the shoes she had worn just a moment ago with my hands. I pressed my lips on one of the jewels while the other substituted as woman during a frenzied fit… This bizarre, mad pleasure seemed to – how should I say? – seemed to lead me straight to Colette herself."

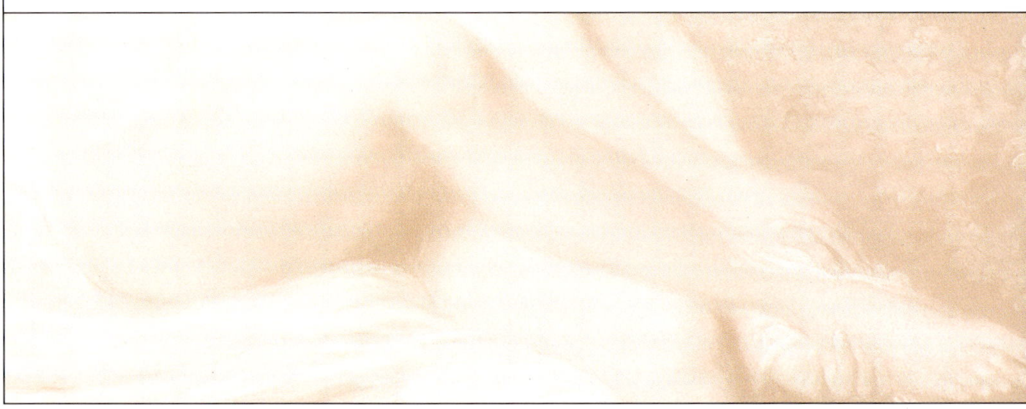

His famous story Fanchette's Foot was
conceived in 1767. One Sunday morning, at the
corner of Montorgueil Street he saw a pretty girl
standing in front of a boutique. She was dressed
in a white slip, silk stockings, and pink shoes
with high stiletto heels.
He was enchanted by what he saw, including the
charming walk of the girl, and in his mind
immediately began writing the first chapter of
the above work, which starts with the words:
"I am the actual historian recording the glorious
conquest of the small foot of a beauty."

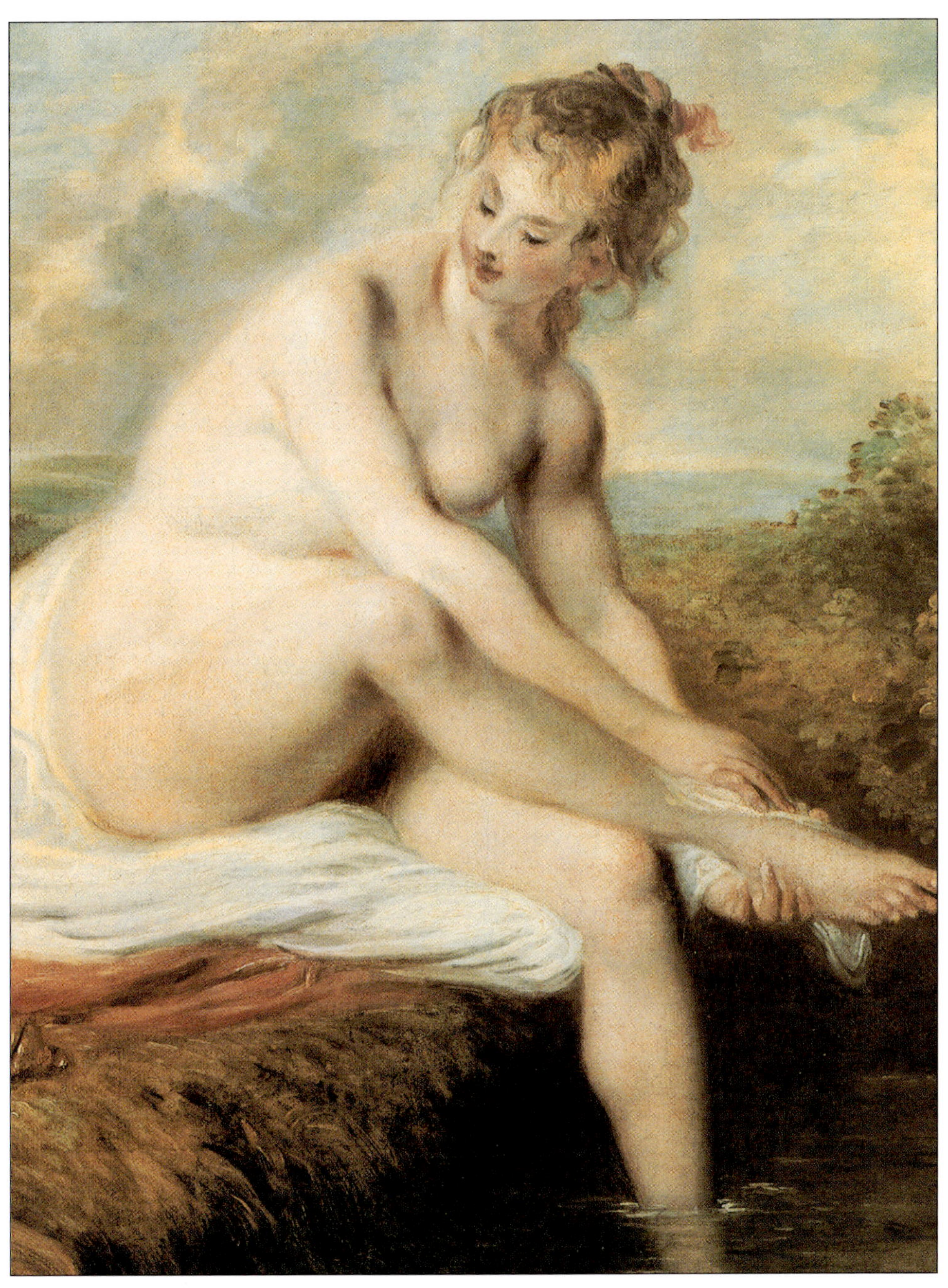

26. Antoine Watteau, Diane au Bain, 1712.

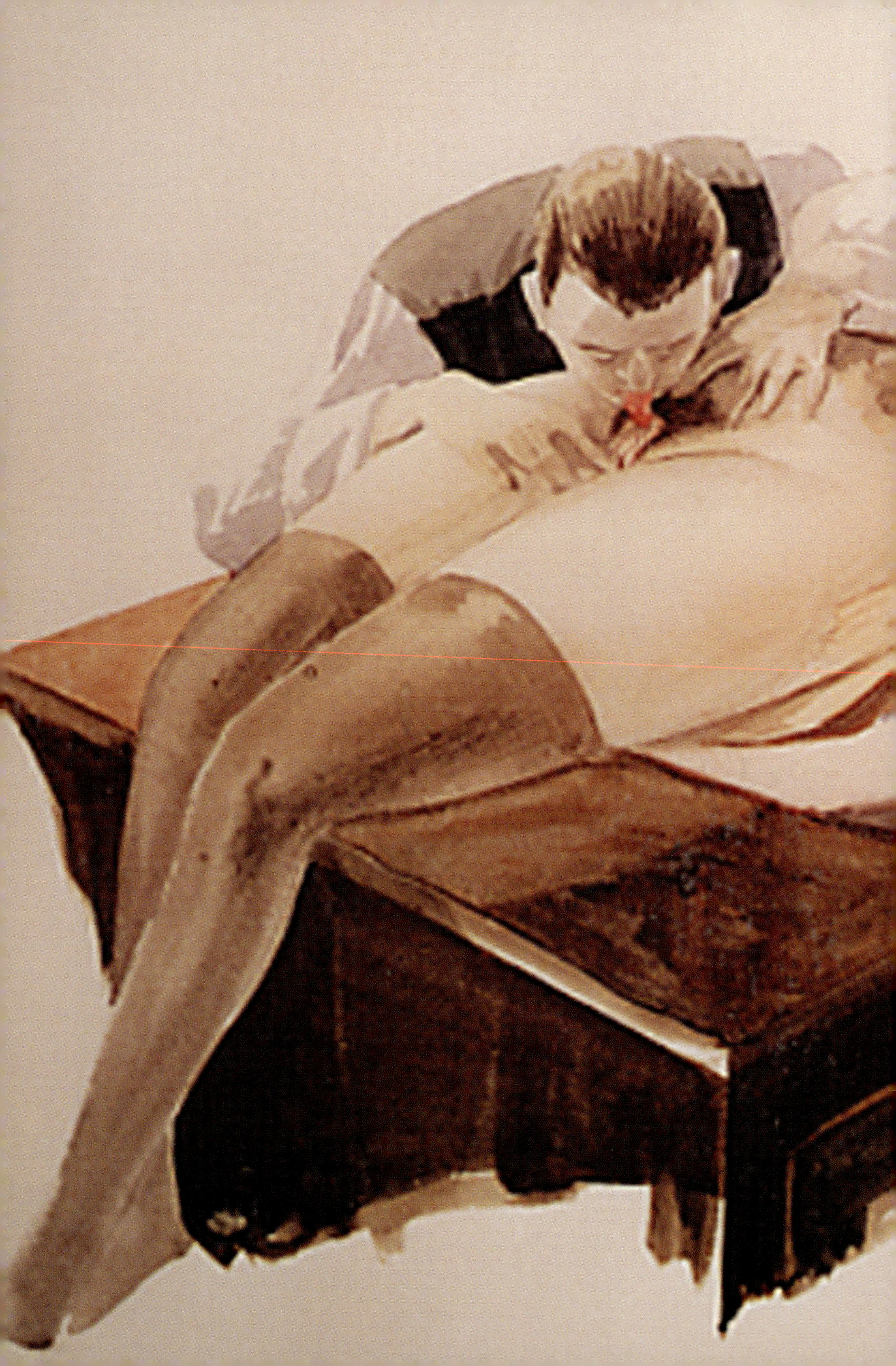

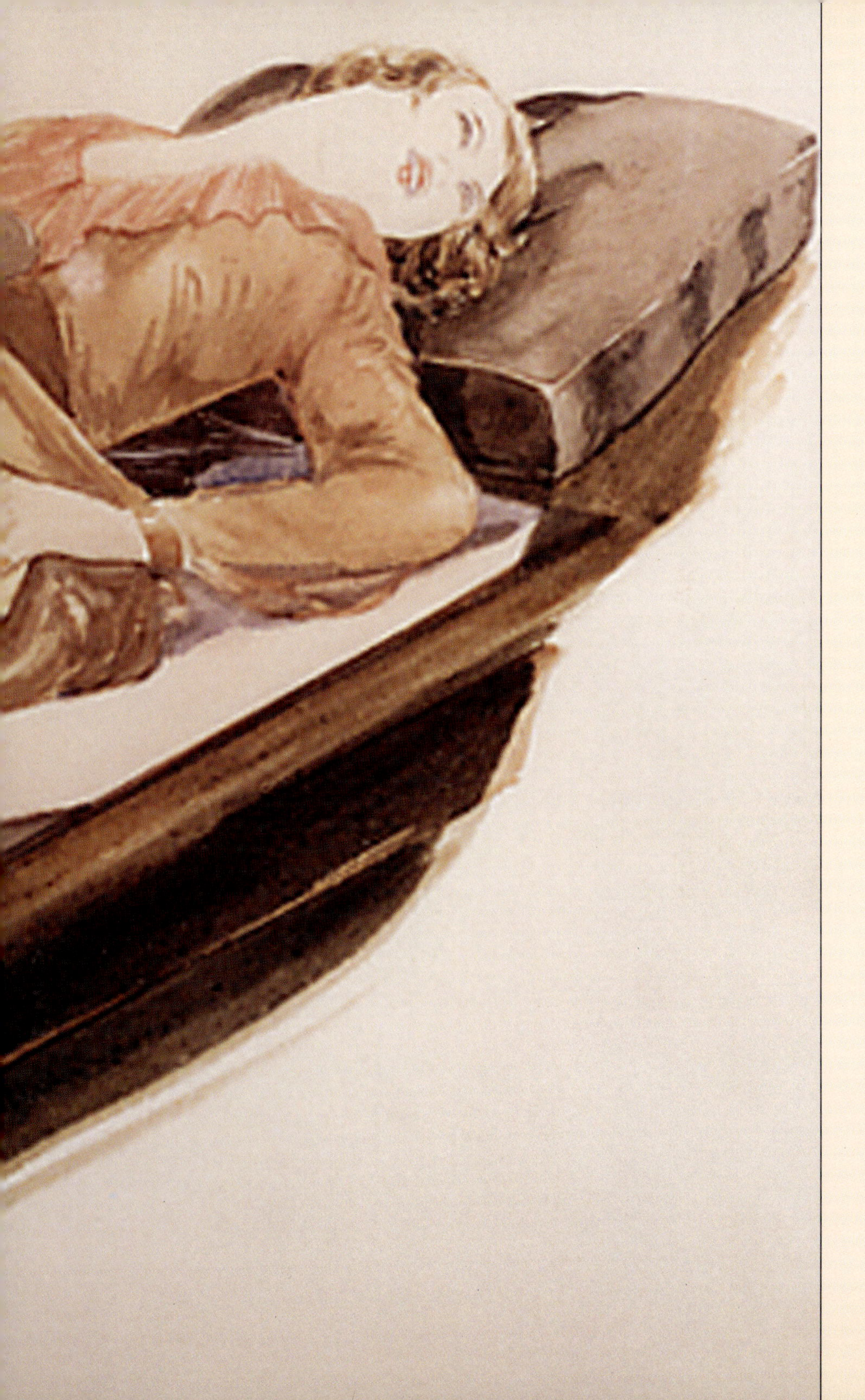

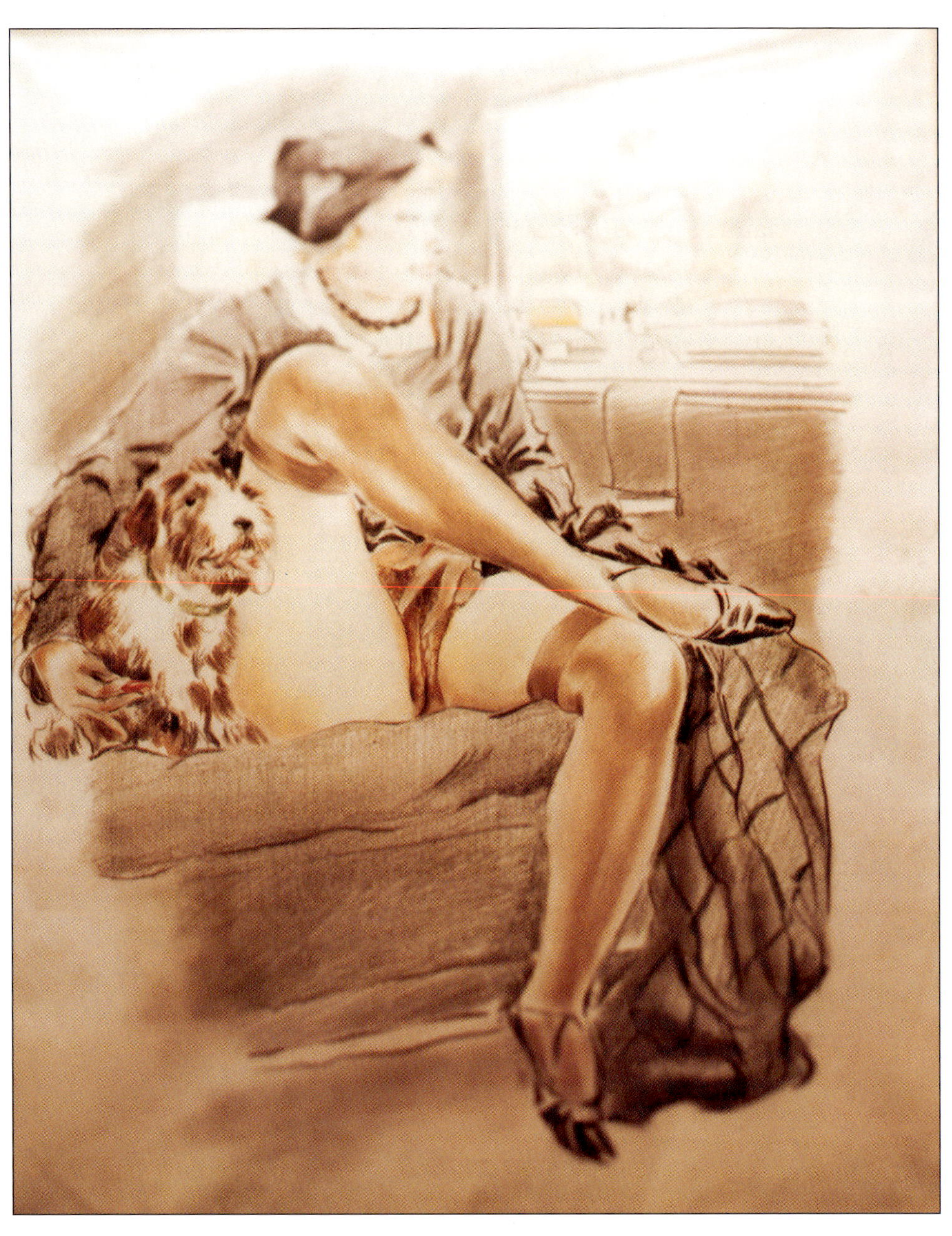

Preceding Pages :
27. Rojan, watercolour, 1925.
28. Rojan, In the Taxi, watercolour, 1930.

The following day, when his imagination had somewhat cooled, he wanted to see his muse once more but instead noticed a woman on Saint-Denis Street whose foot was a "miracle of daintiness" dressed in a delightful gold-trimmed shoe made by the premier shoemaker of Paris. Full of enthusiasm he hurried home and in two days wrote the first 14 chapters of Pied de Fanchette.

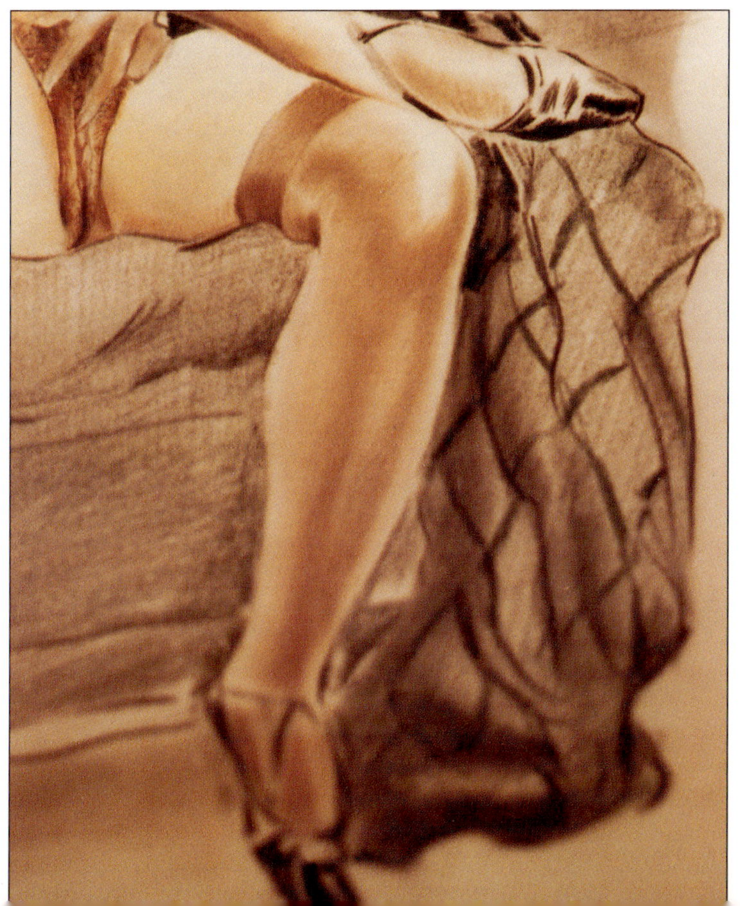

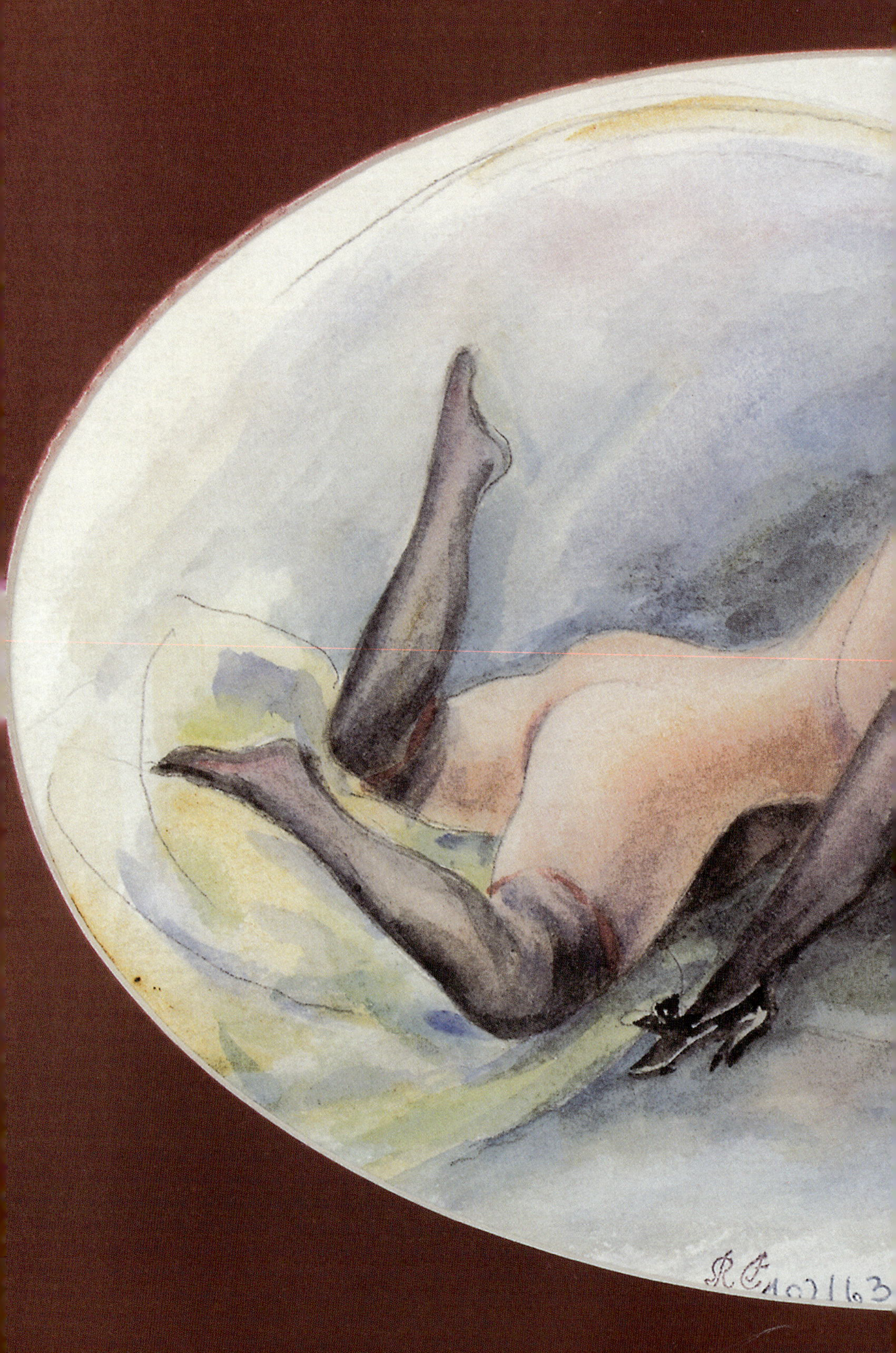

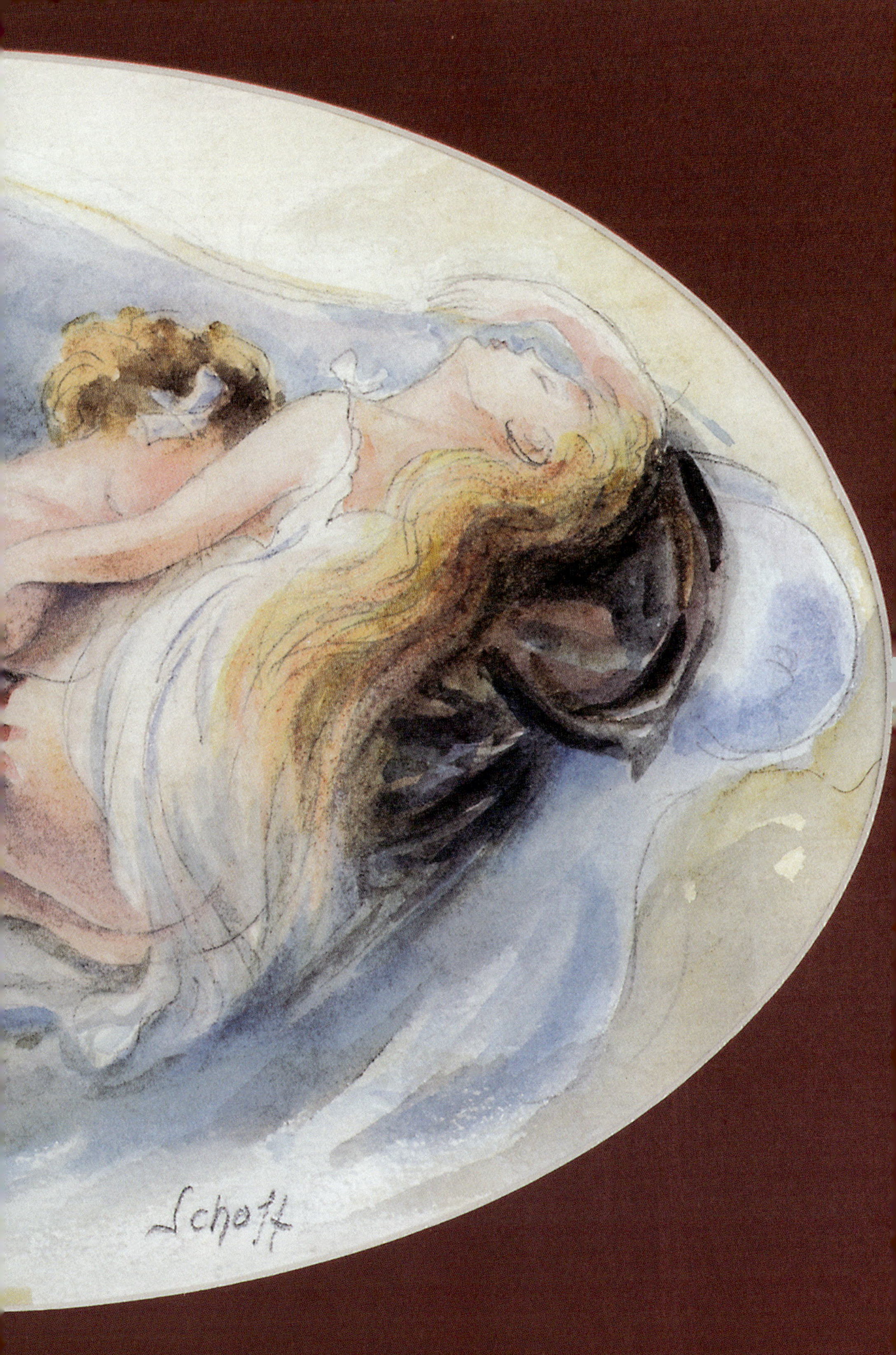
Schoff

A friend reports about Rétif: "Our dear Nicolas had a rather strange but I believe excusable obsession. No matter how ugly a woman's face was, whether she was hunchbacked or limped, our dear friend always fell madly in love with her if she had a pretty foot and especially if she wore pretty shoes. He relished a woman's feet more than anything; they were everything for him in terms of bliss and pleasure." The woman herself was viewed as a somewhat insignificant appendix of her foot or her shoes.

In his eyes, the dainty shoe made these women divine: "If one were to show a savage who has never seen a woman wear a shoe a lady's shoe crafted by the shoemaker Bourbon who lives on Vieux-Augustins Street, and were to ask this savage what kind of creature would wear this object, he would surely answer: 'An angel, a fairy, a sylph!'"

There is nothing worse than the heavy flat foot coming in contact with the dirt of the earth.

Preceding Pages :
29. Otto Schoff, lithograph, around 1930.
30. Anonymous drawing, 1922.

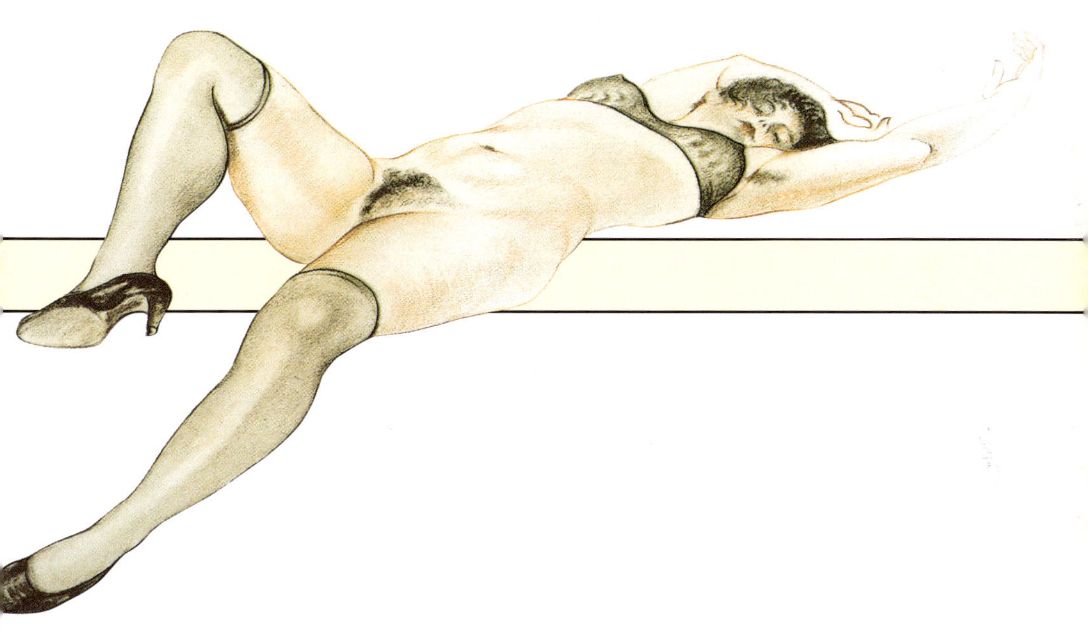

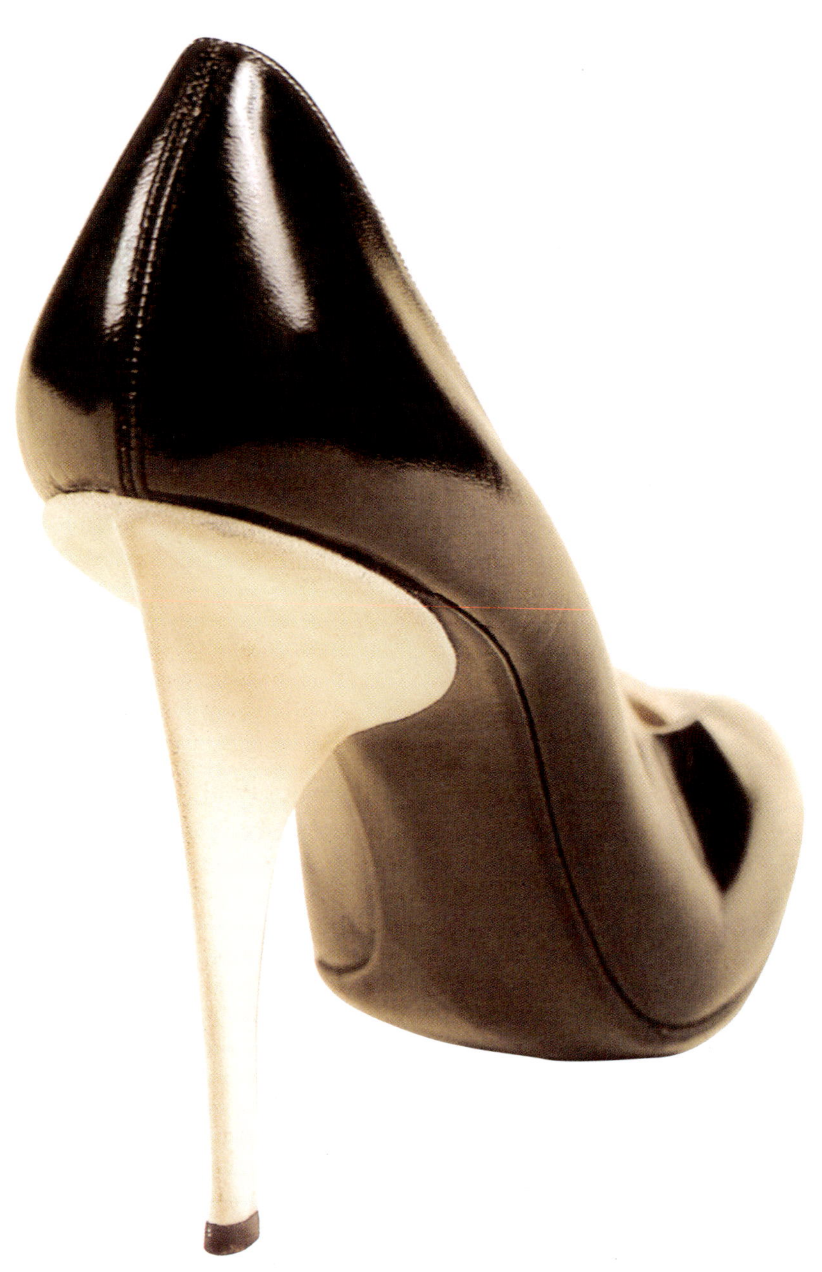

31. Fashion-design, Perugia, 1920s.

*I*n Monsieur Nicolas he heavily criticized the "low-heeled shoes of the female republicans" and was angry at the newspapers that promoted this ugly fashion trend. The foot and shoe fetish is Rétif's primary sexual perversion in life. Since he was the first to describe this variation of fetishism in detail, the German sexologist Iwan Bloch suggested calling the shoe and foot fetishism "Retifism" – applying the same logic that derived the term "sadism" from Sade and "masochism" from Sacher-Masoch.

Literature mentions foot fetishism quite early. Brantôme writes in his work Lives of the Gallant Ladies (1665) that Lucius Vitellius, father of emperor Vitellius, supposedly had been a shoe and foot fetishist. He reports that he asked empress Messalina one day for her permission to wear her shoes. "After he had worn them, he kept one and always carried it with him under his shirt and kissed it as often as he could and by adoring the shoe adored his beloved since neither her natural foot nor her pretty legs was available to him."

Brantôme declared this piece of clothing more sensual than nudity itself. "The foot has to be slipped into a pretty, white shoe, a shoe made of black or colored velvet, or a pretty little shoe with a stiletto heel." He considered an average-sized foot as more beautiful than a very large or very small foot. Such a foot is especially seductive if its wearer "moves and shakes it with small little turns and kicks" and if covered by a "pretty little shoe with stiletto heels, white and pointed at the front, not square."

French fashion of the 18th century finally picked up this impression and systematically used it while discovering the charms of the female foot.

32. Margit Gaal, lithograph, 1921.

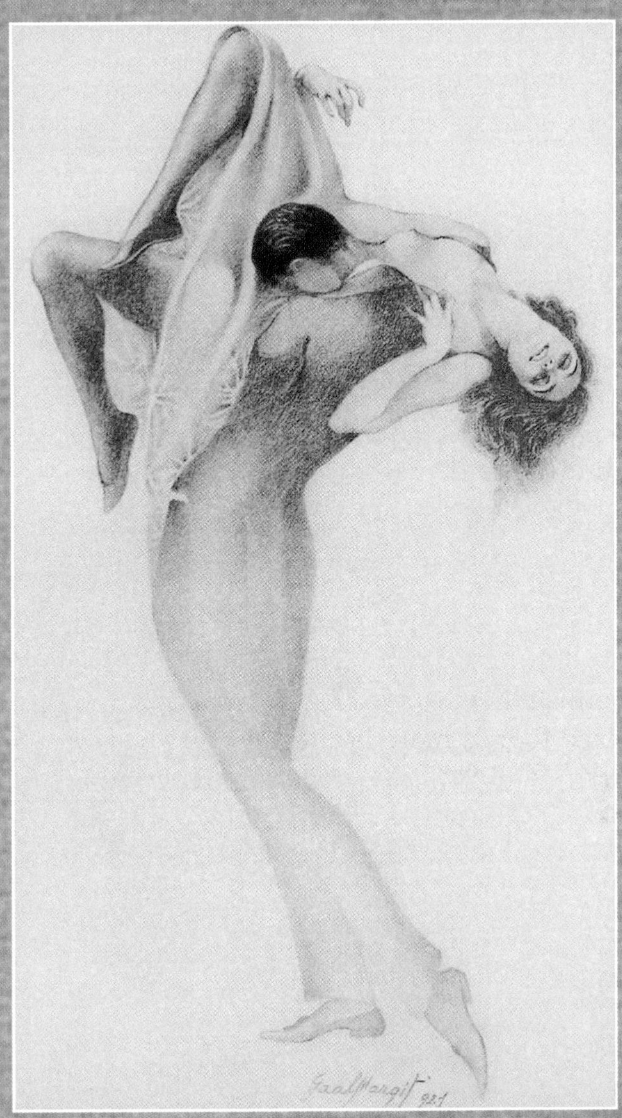

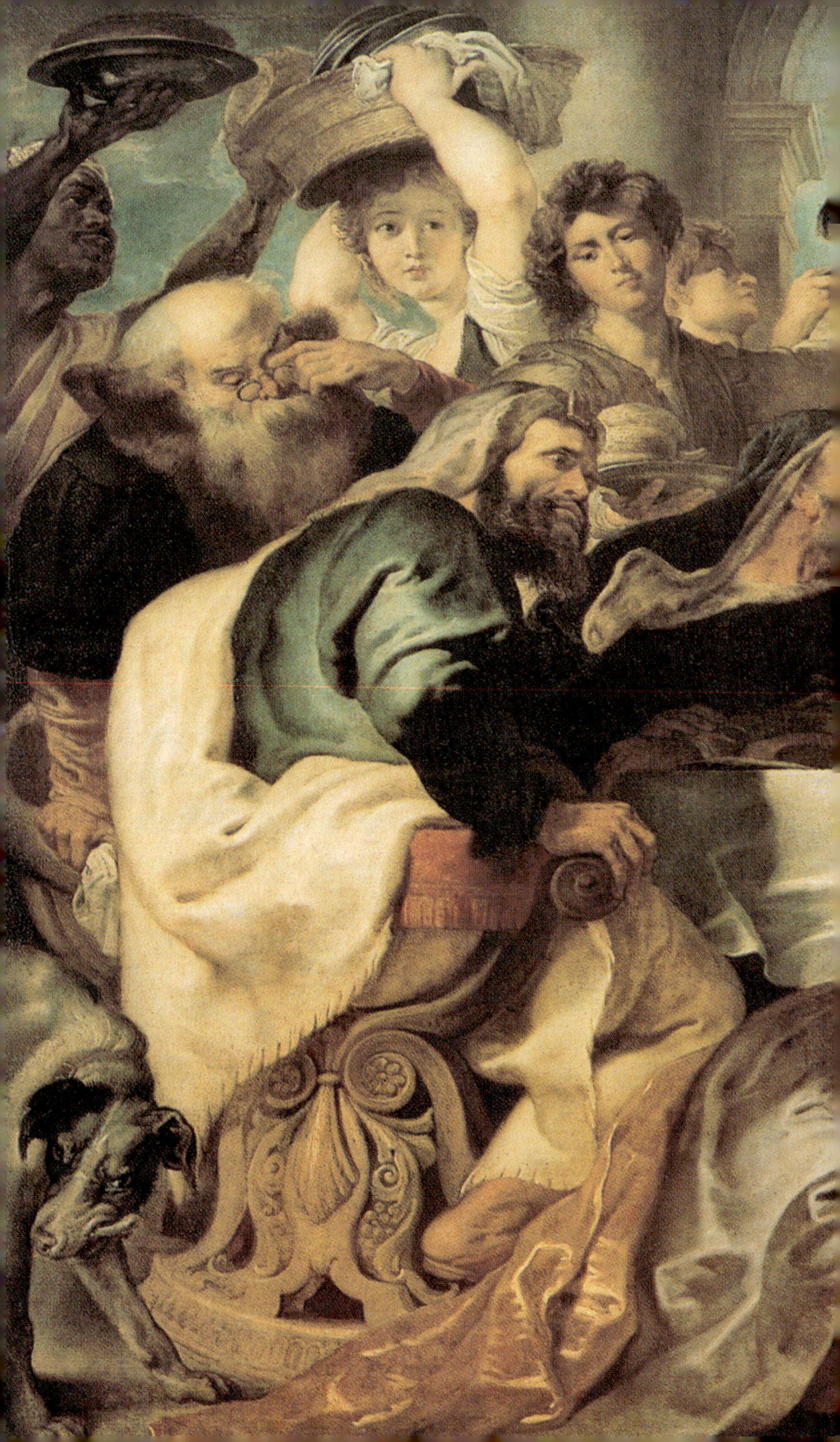

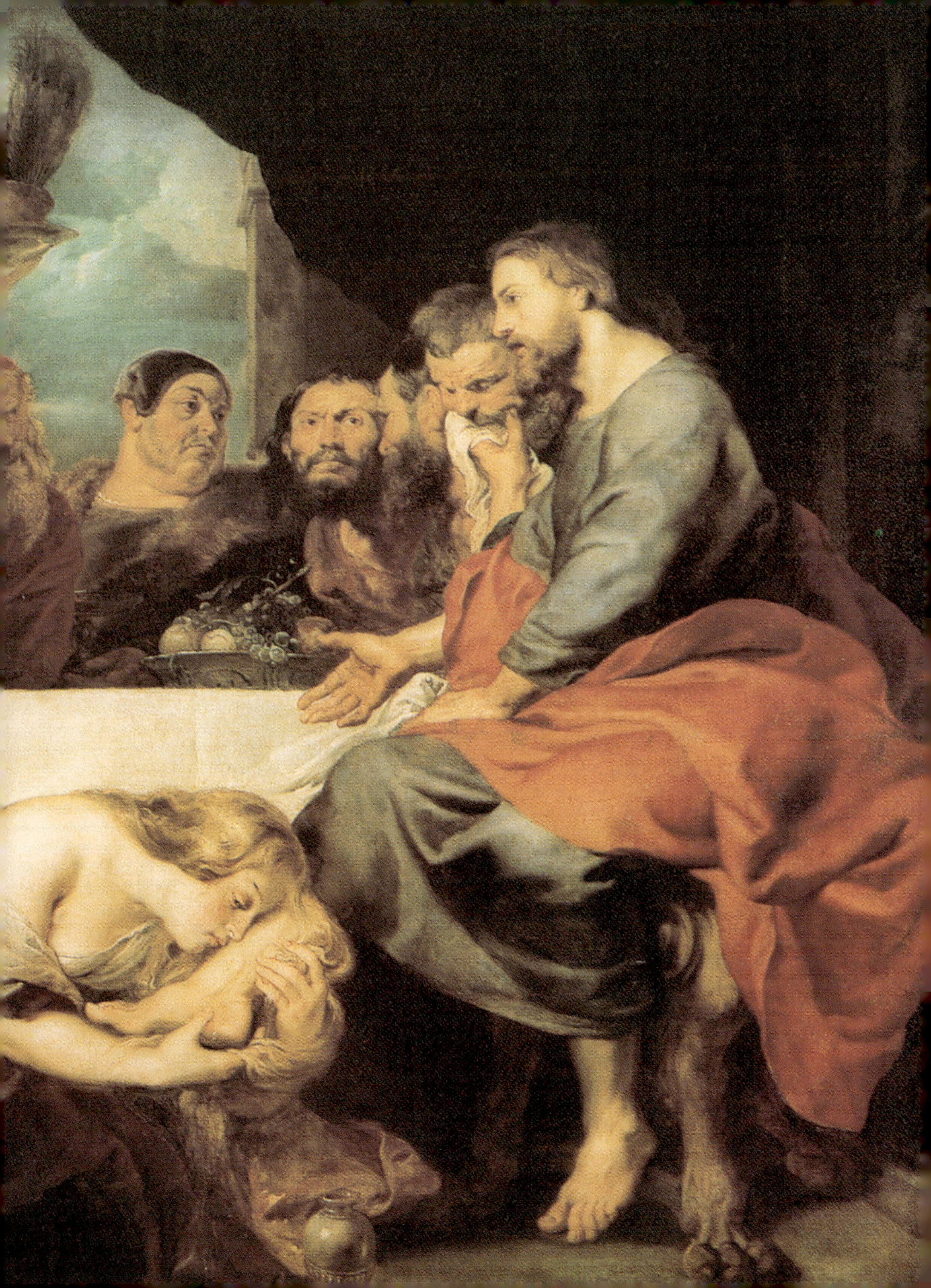

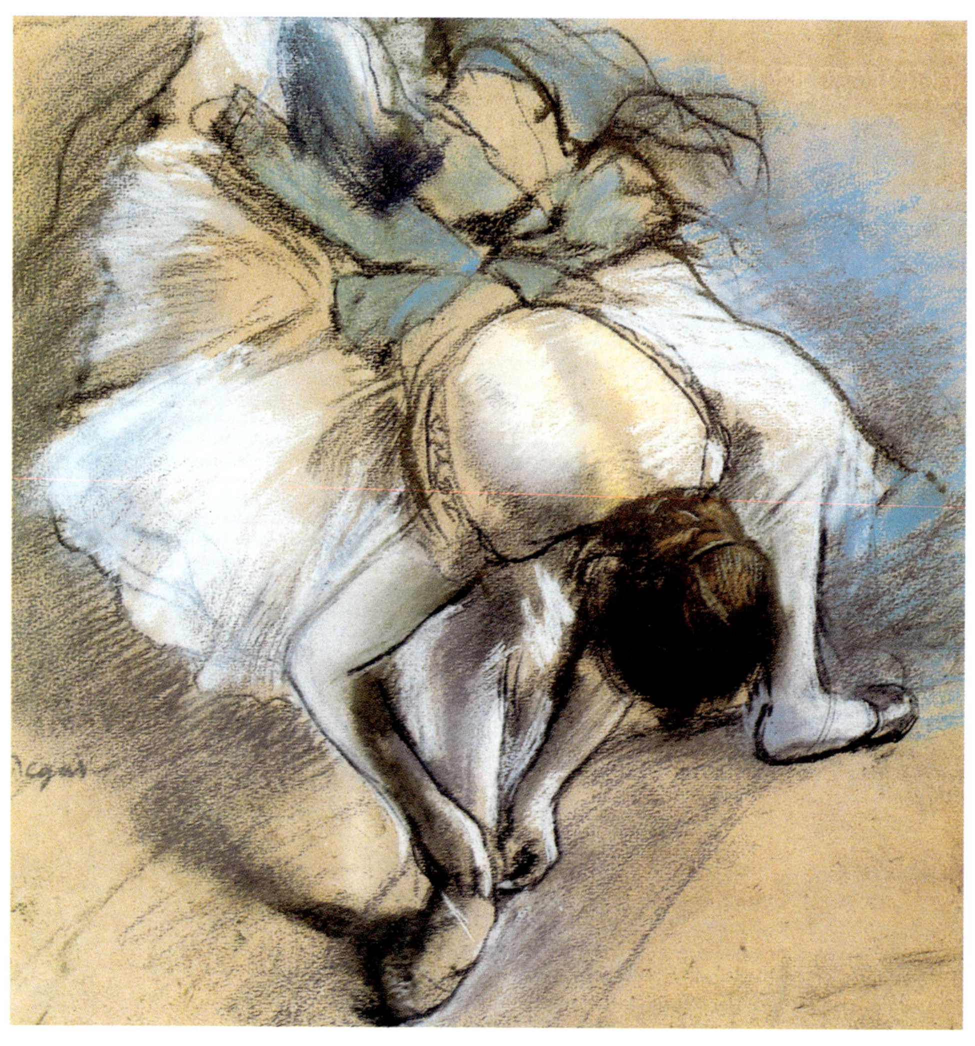

33. Peter Paul Rubens, The Meal at the House of Simon the Pharisee, around 1620.
34. Edgar Degas, Dancer Adjusting Her Shoe, 1880–1885.

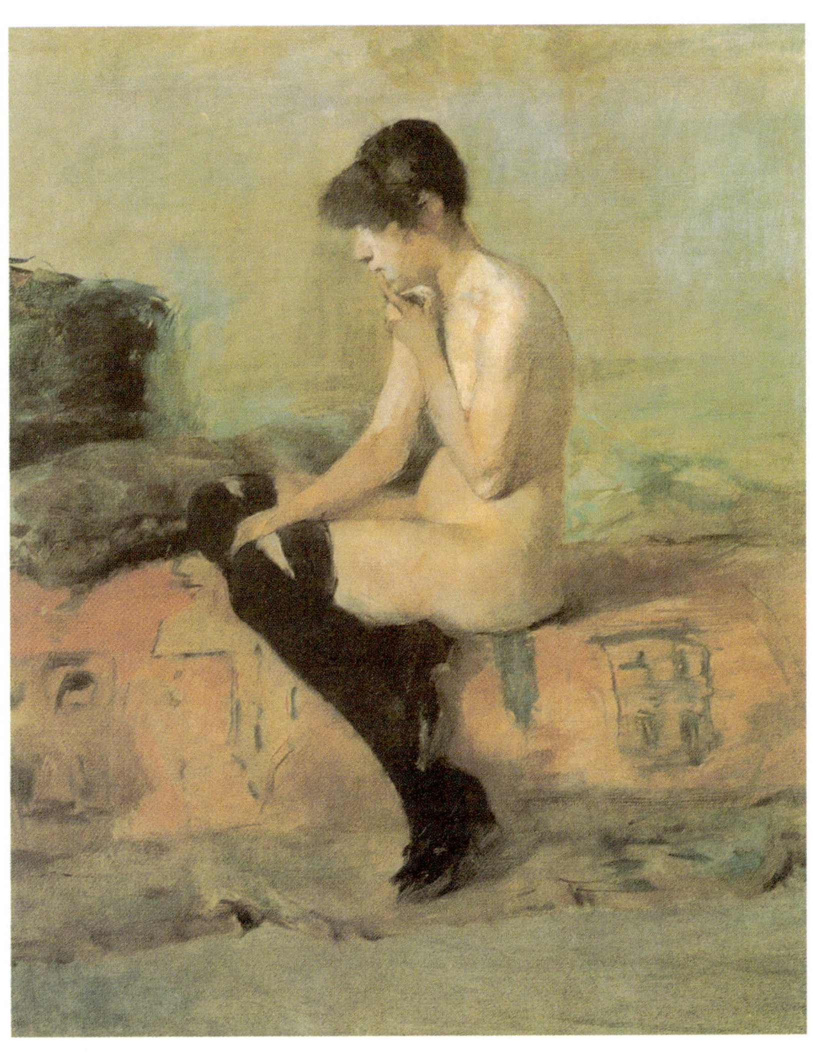

35. Henri de Toulouse-Lautrec, Nude Study, 1883.

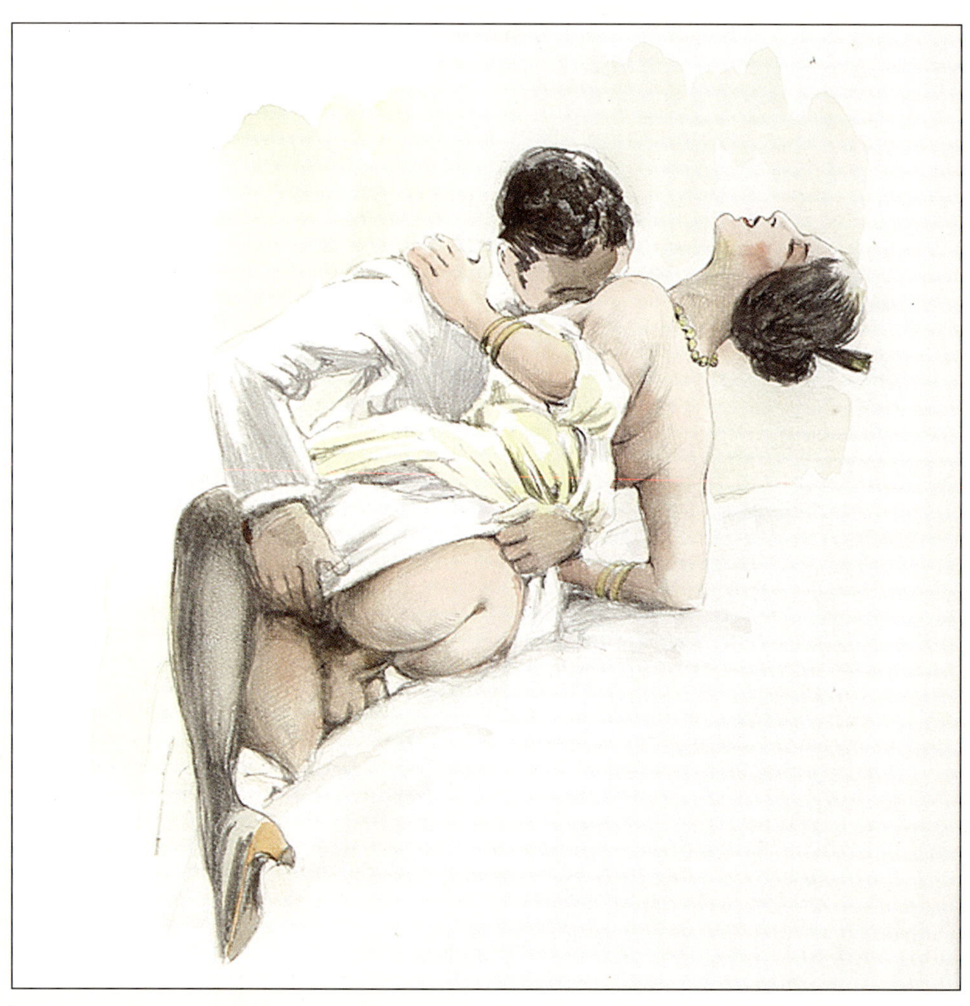

36. Couple in Natural Surroundings, watercolour, American, 1930s.

*W*as Goethe a Foot Fetishist?
On 14 July 1803 Goethe wrote to Christiane during his long absence: "Next chance you have, send me your latest new shoes, the ones that are already worn from too much dancing you described to me so that I once again have something of you close to me to press to my heart. Farewell!" This individual case is often cited as proof of Goethe's foot fetishism. The significant role this fetishism played in his life and work cannot be denied, however. His work Wilhelm Meister is an excellent source for the continuation of this subject. In Wahlverwandtschaften [Elective Affinities] he writes: "He threw himself down at her feet and she was unable to prevent him from kissing her shoes and grasping her foot to press it tenderly against his chest."

Still, Eisler felt some reservations about Goethe being a shoe fetishist as he expressed in his psychoanalytical study of Goethe: "He voiced his request to Christiane only once and that should be a deterrent from assuming with certainty that this perversion was a part of Goethe's life."

Already Rétif wondered about the causes of this strange inclination. "Does this preference for pretty feet, which is so strong in me that it always arouses my lust and let's me forget any other ugliness, has its roots in a psychological or intellectual natural disposition? The passion for pretty foot wear I have since childhood was an acquired inclination based on a natural predisposition."

Sigmund Freud recognized the symbolic significance of the foot and linked it with early childhood. "The fetishistic veneration of the female
foot and shoe seems to use the foot only as a
substitute symbol for the once venerated, since
then sorely missed, penis of the woman; the
"cutter off of braids" play, without knowing it,
the role of persons performing the act of castration of the female genitalia." This means it is the
fixation on the urgently desired object, the penis
of the woman, which leaves indelible tracks in
the emotional life of the child.

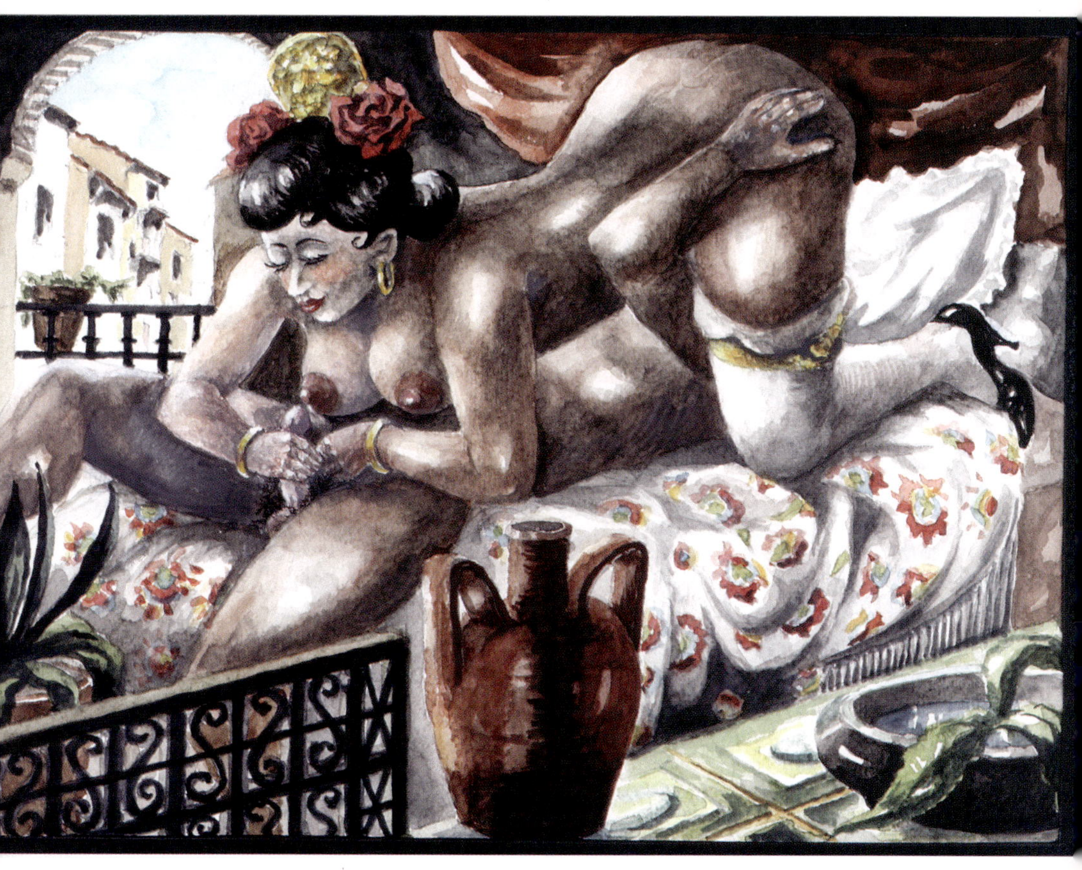

37. De Monceau, watercolour, around1940.

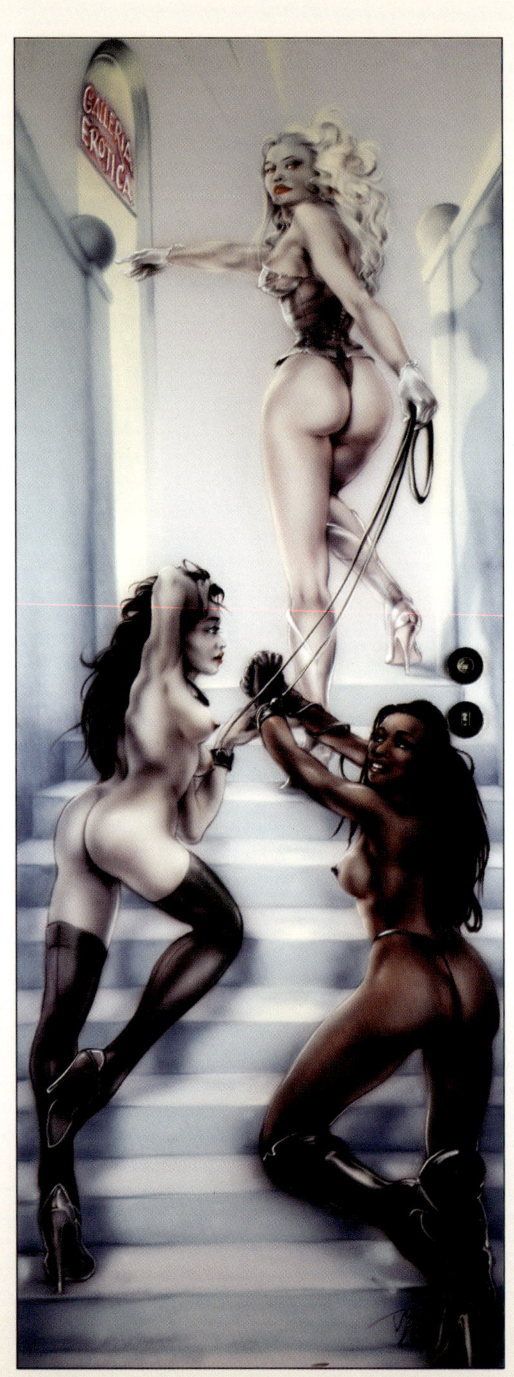
GALLERIA
EROTICA

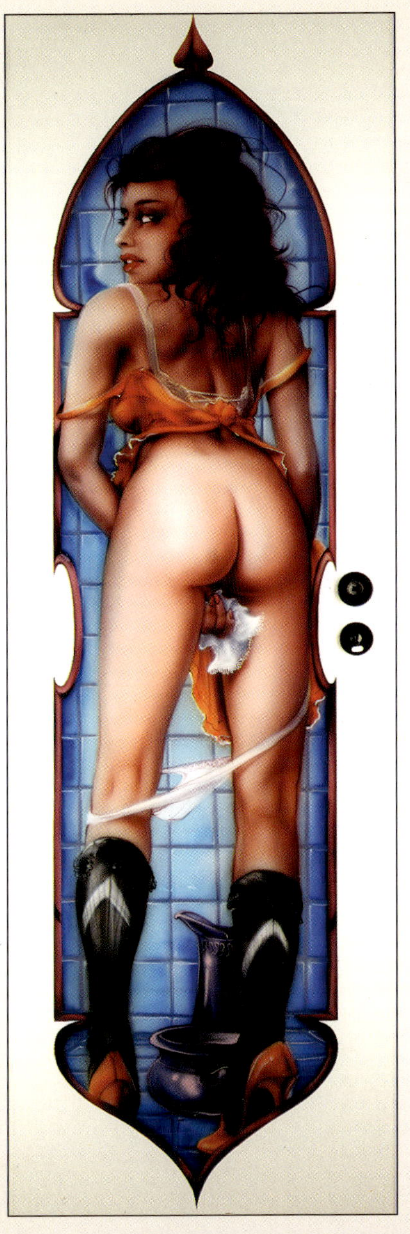

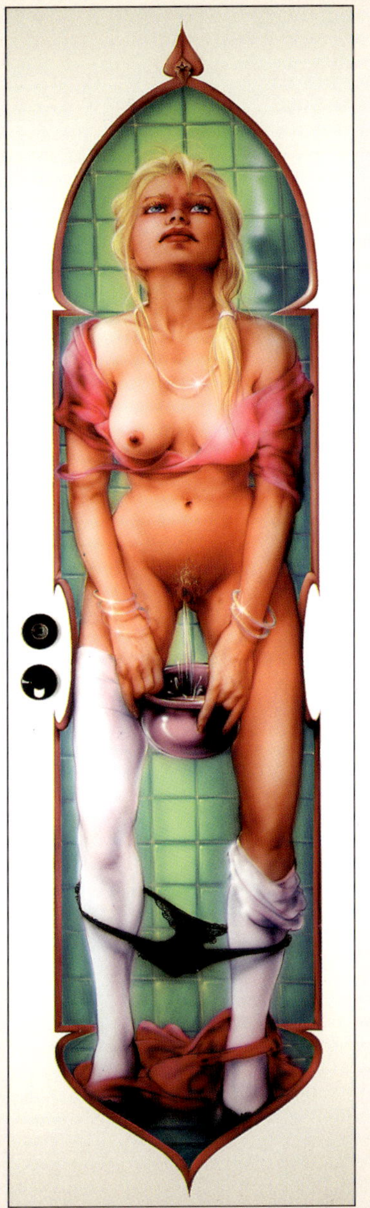

38. Joe Brockerhoff, aerograph.
39. Joe Brockerhoff, aerograph.
40. Joe Brockerhoff, aerograph.

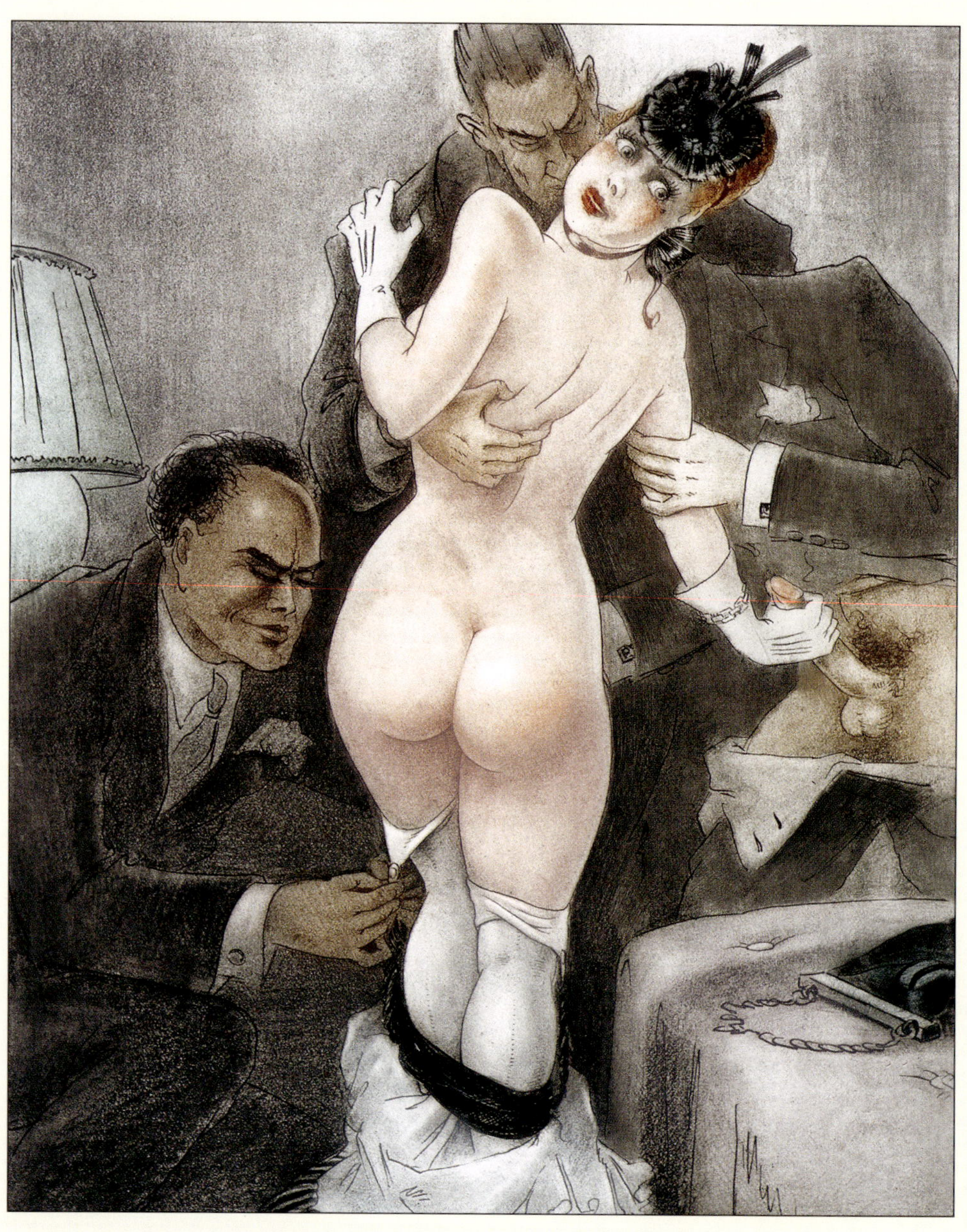

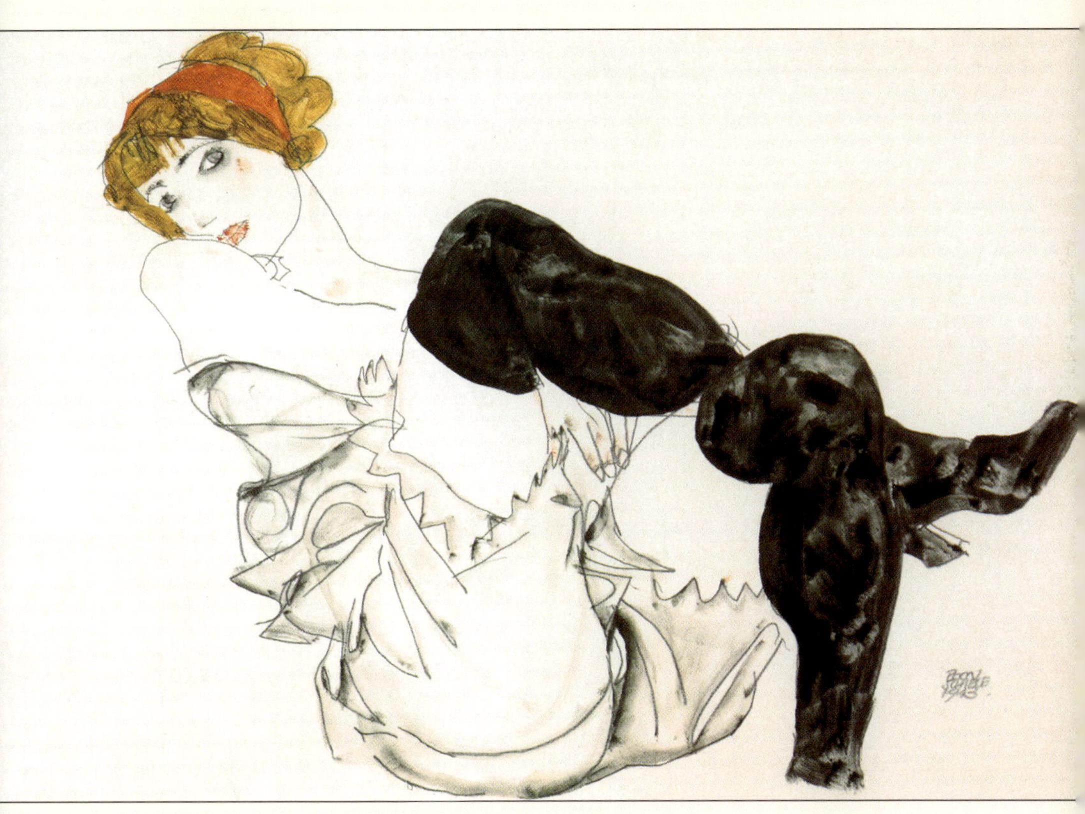

41. Jean Morisot, colour engraving, 1925.
42. Egon Schiele, Woman in Black Stockings, 1913.

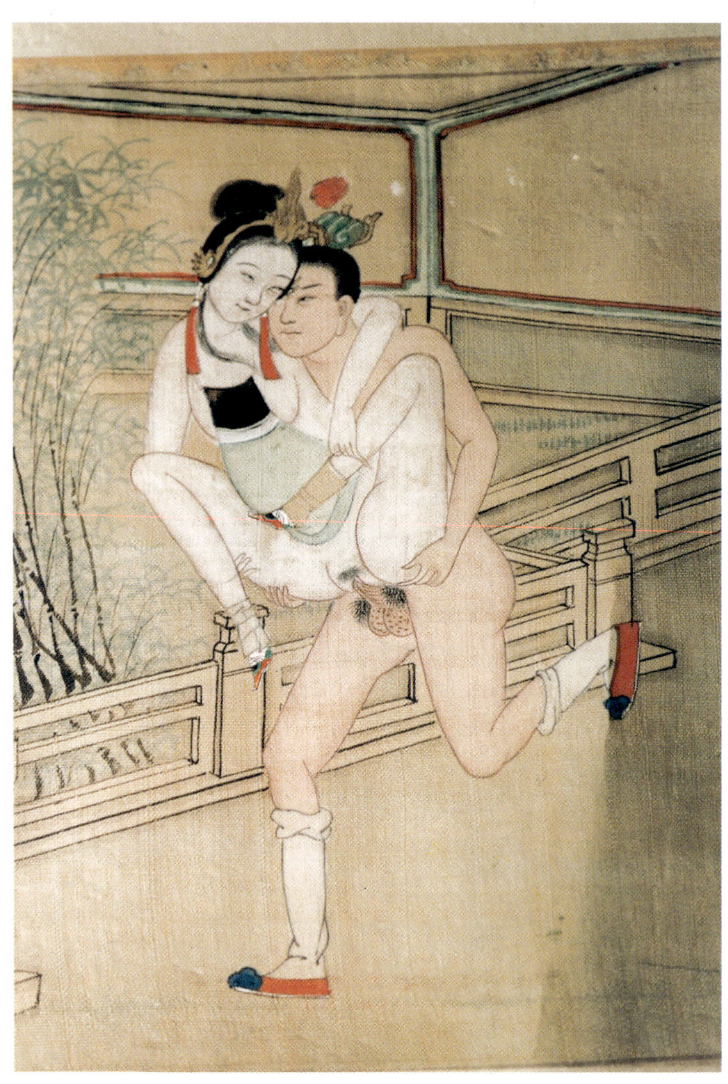

43. Wedding book, probably Japanese, 19th century.

Freud's essay about W. Jensen's Gradiva analyzes the interest of the young archeologist Norbert Hanold in the feet and foot positions of female individuals. Hanold has no interest in the living, breathing woman. He has shifted this interest to woman made of stone or bronze. "When suitable, our poet imbues his hero with a lively interest in the walk and foot positions of women, which has to lead to him falling into disrepute as a foot fetishist – with science as with the women of his home – which, however, is derived from the memory of this female childhood playmate. Already as a child, this girl exhibits a beautiful walk with an almost vertically placed tip of the foot when walking and by describing this walk, an antique stone relief Norbert Hanold discovers later gains said significance for him. We should add that the poet is in full agreement with the sciences when attributing the peculiar phenomenon of fetishism to early childhood. Since A. Binet we have been really trying to link fetishism with erotic childhood events and impressions." This means that fetishism offers a symbolic, mental link leading to the substitution of the object, namely the female penis.

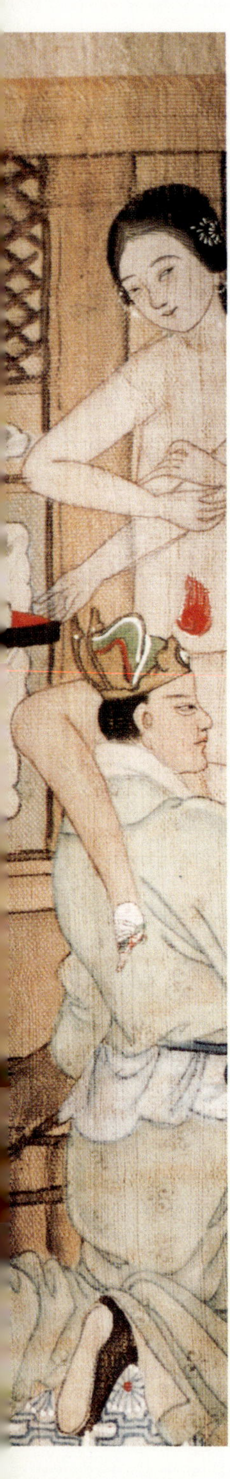

Freud mentions the binding and subsequent mutilation of the female foot in ancient China: "First, the foot is mutilated, then it is venerated. One could think that the Chinese man thanks the woman for submitting to castration."
The foot is an age-old sexual symbol, already mentioned in myths. The shoe or slipper thus became the symbol of the female genitalia.

44. Wedding book, probably Japanese, 19th century.
45. Coloured shunga ('Images of Spring'), silk on card, 18th century.
46. Coloured shunga ('Images of Spring'), silk on card, 18th century.

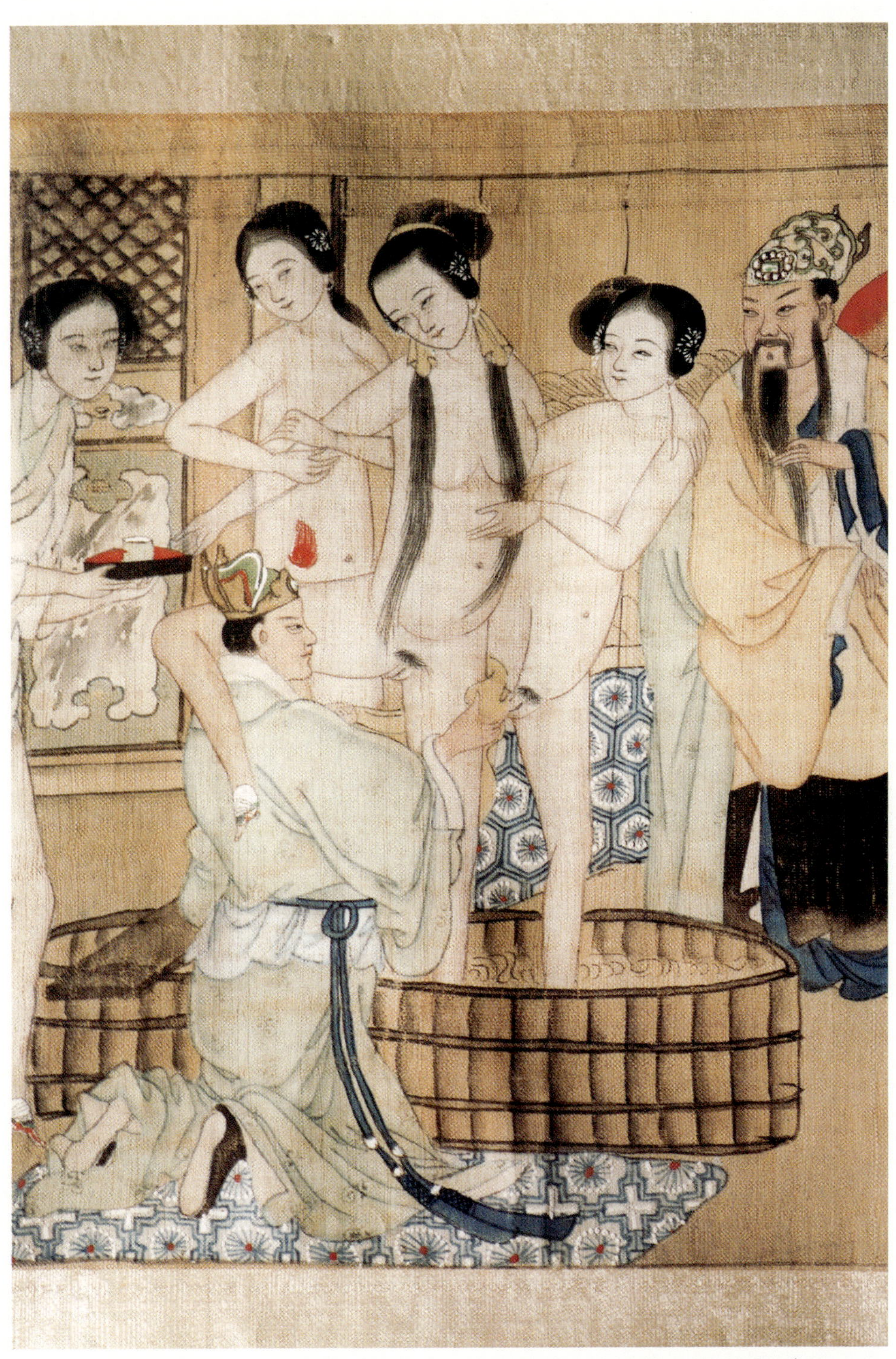

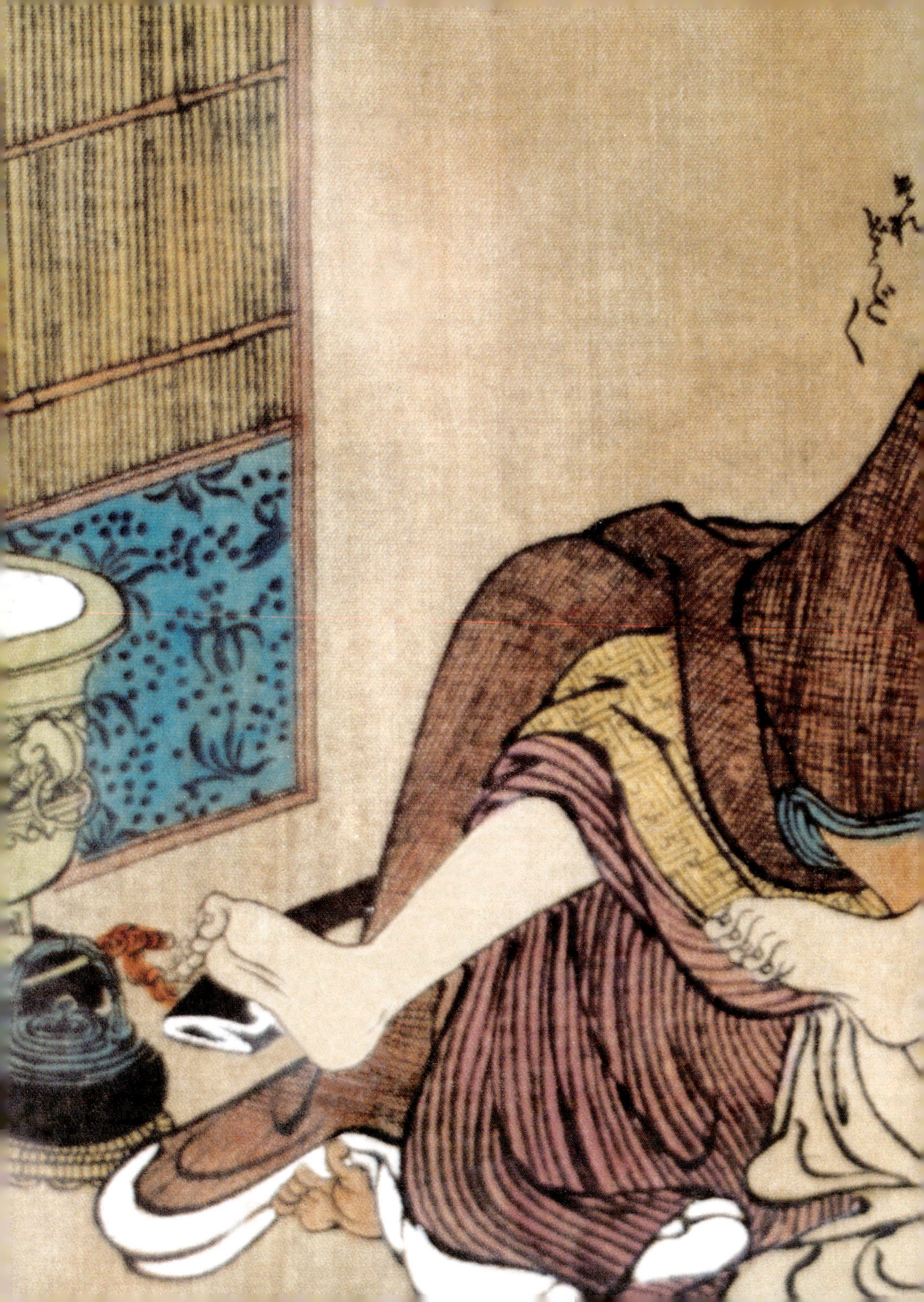

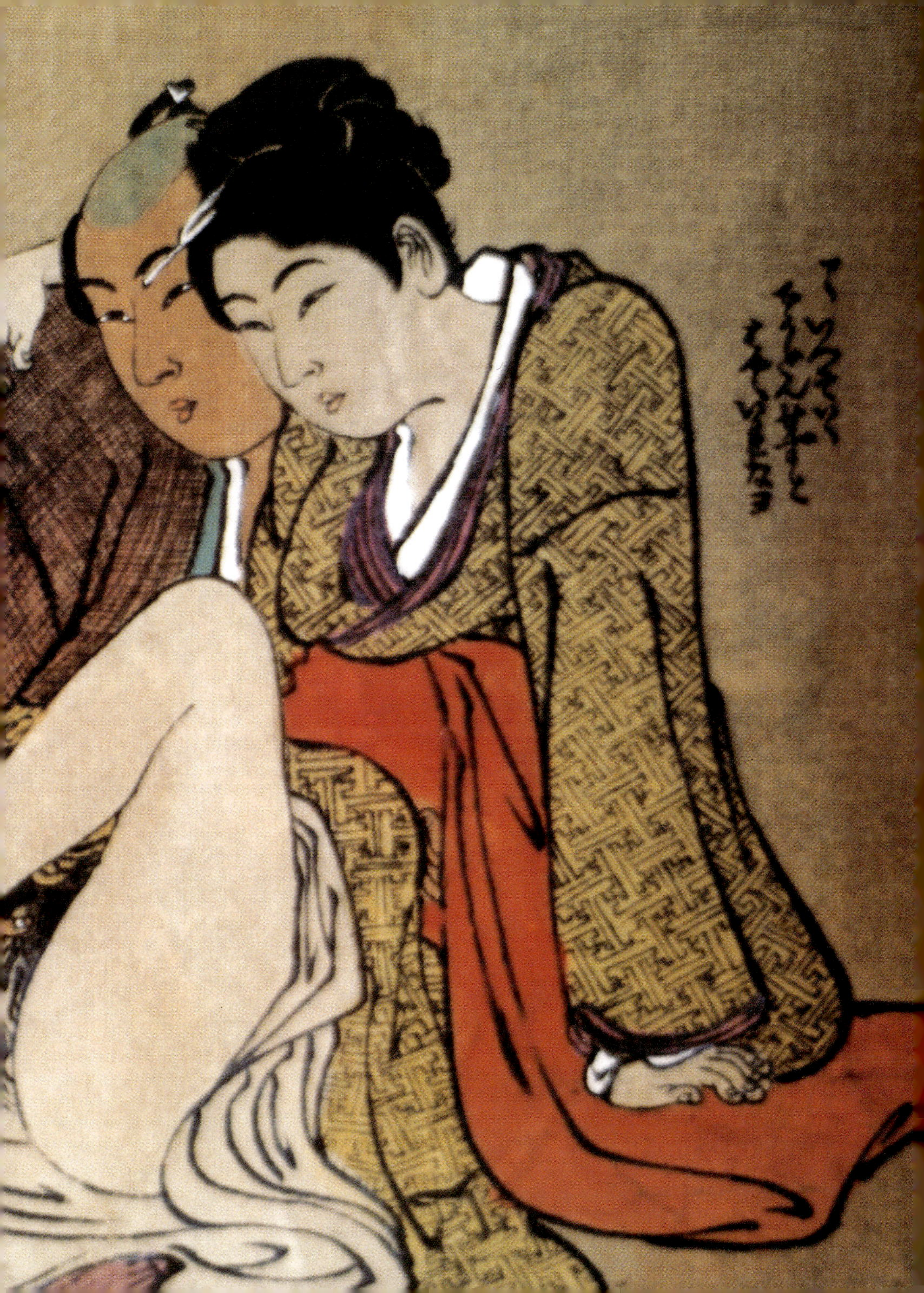

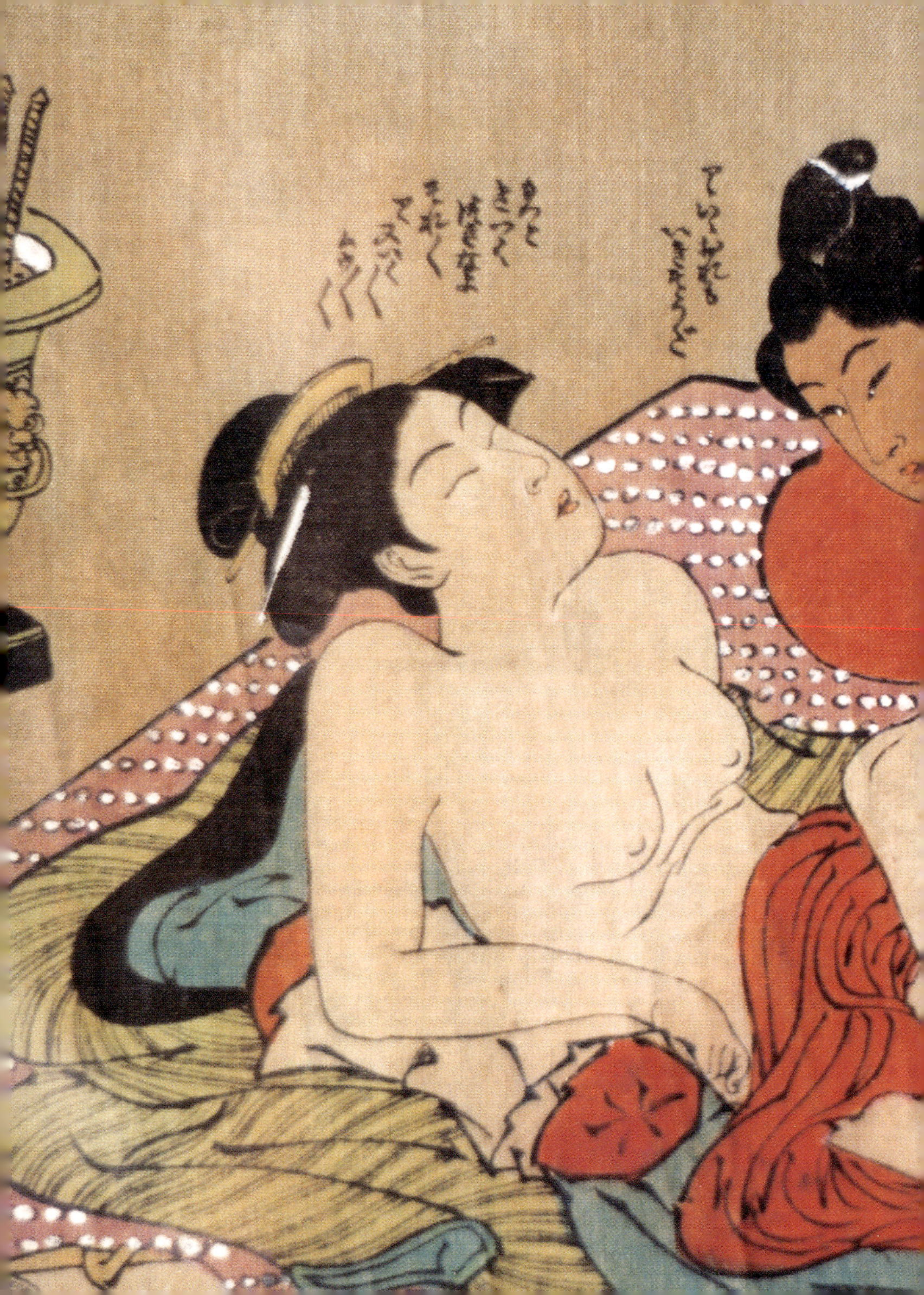

あはと
きつく
はきそ
まれ
くくく
と
てらゝ花も
ひゝゝと

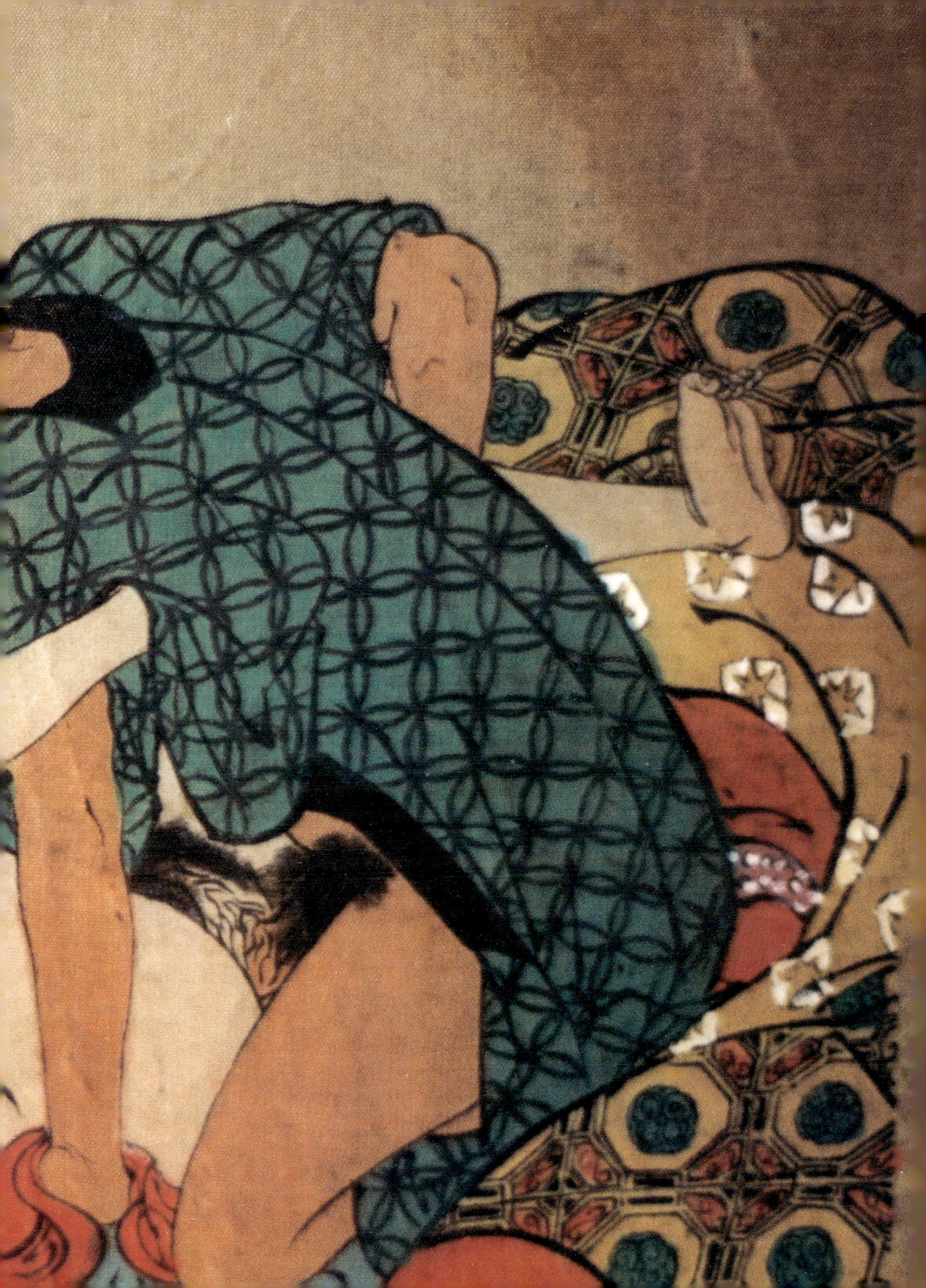

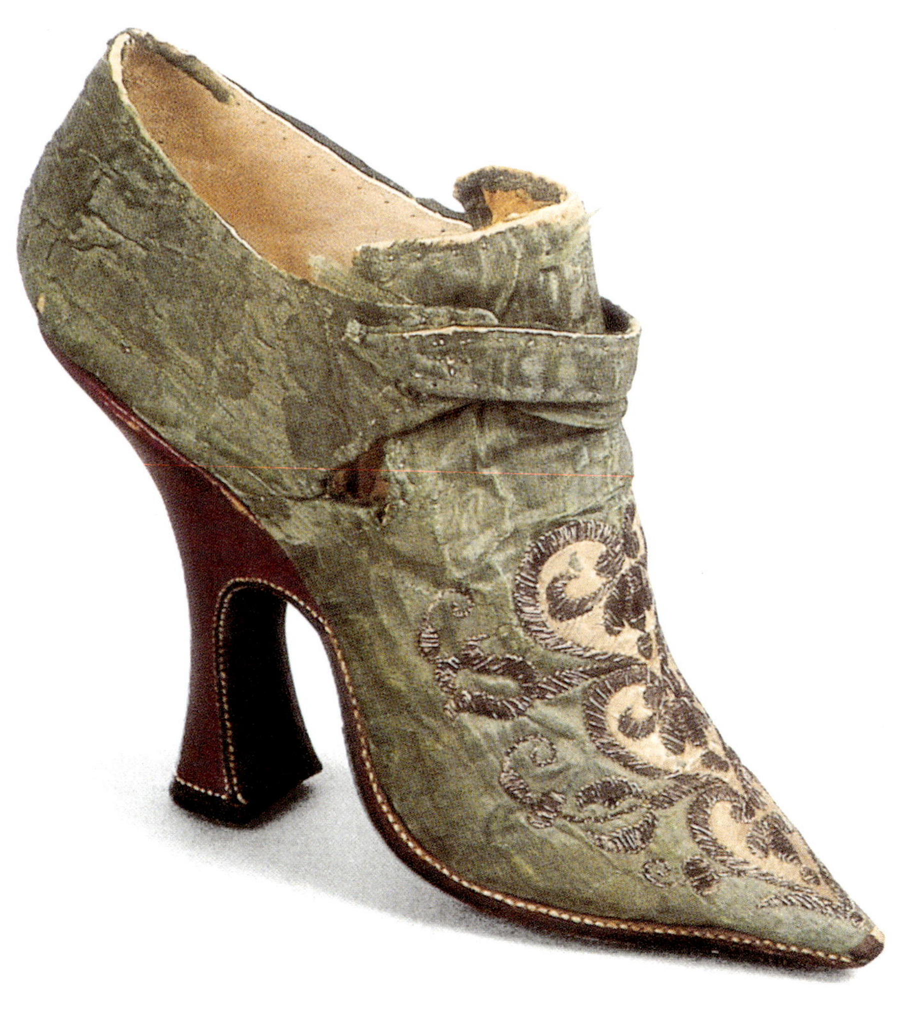

47. Woman's shoe, London, 1720.

In his 1914 book Marias jungfräuliche Mutterschaft [Mary's Virginal Motherhood], A. J. Storfer refers to the fairytale of Cinderella: "The prince sees her shoe (vulva) and is so delighted with its smallness and daintiness that he searches for its owner and marries her. Cinderella, who has a "small shoe," is the proper counterpart to the youngest brother who has a "large sword."
The Cinderella motif can already be found in the ancient tales about the beautiful Rodopis. An eagle – the symbolic animal of patriarchic sexuality – stole one of her sandals while she bathed and brought it to Memphis to the king. The king, delighted with the daintiness of the sandal, searched for its owner to marry her.

The soft sandal might also represent the vagina; the shoe with stiletto heel, however, combines vaginal and phallic meaning. The dream reported to us in 1905 by the writer Franziska Countess of Reventlov is especially illustrative of the phallic significance:

"Tonight - dreamed twice of shoes with stiletto heels - I accompanied myself to a restaurant and did not know how to refer to myself. Thought quite confused: should I say 'my wife" or 'he'?" A confusion of sexual identity. What is interesting about this dream is that it is not the imagination of a man, as it is usually the case, who has to deal with his castration complex. It is also interesting that women have a tendency towards such substitutions. Just looking at the vast quantity of shoes many women own.

Has the foot and shoe fetishism lost its potency in our era of short skirts? Certainly not. Early childhood fantasies do not change with the fashions. Only their subsequent execution and costume utilize the store of available options.

48. Anonymous etching, Paris, around 1920.

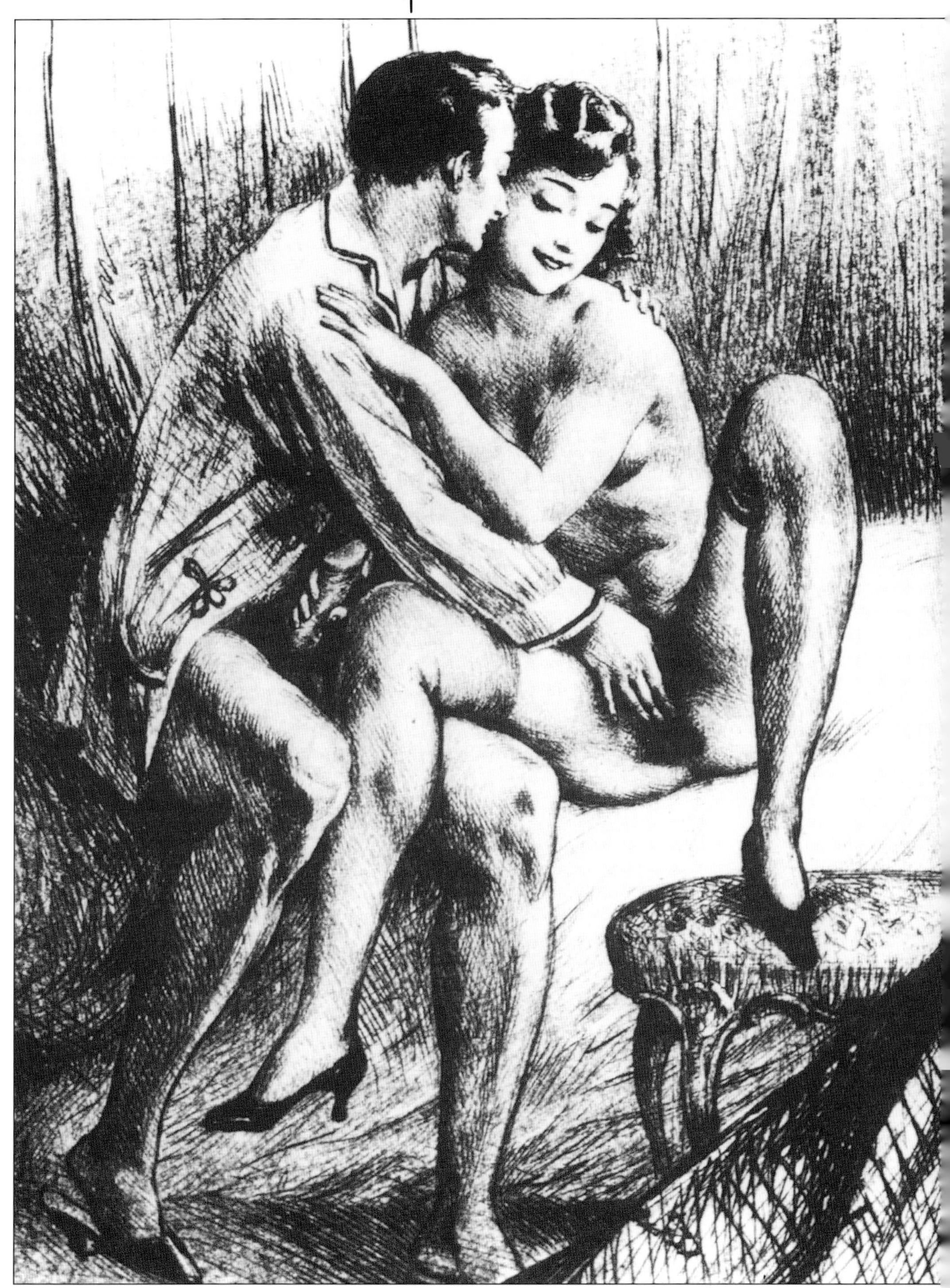

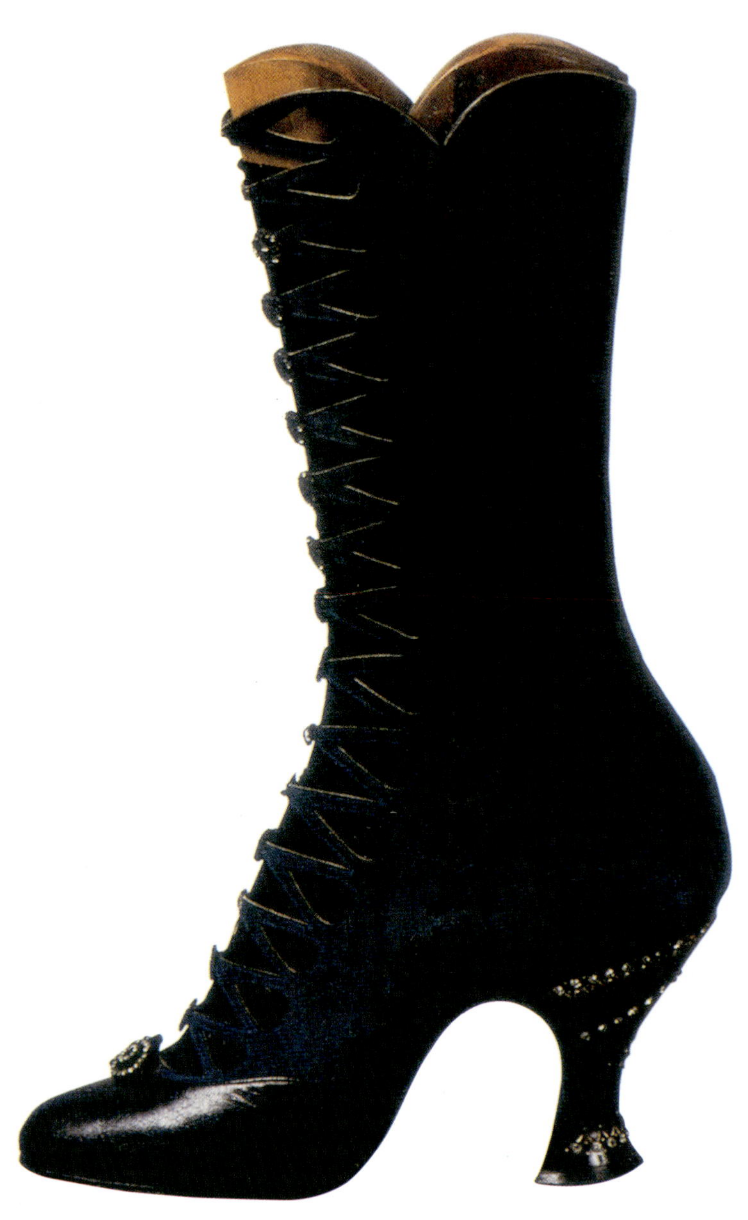

49. Boot with laces, 1890.

The fact that we continue to be born by mothers and we have to find our sexual identity with and against them is enough cause for stumbling long before fashion could exert any influence over us. It is a piece of "recherche du temps perdu" [Remembrance of Things Past, but re-translated recently and more accurately as In Search of Lost Time] that is frozen within all variations of fetishism.

Every madam of a bordello can still today tell stories of "shoe Johns" and "foot Johns." For example, D. – owner-operator of a Frankfurt luxury bordello – told me of a client who always arrived with a suitcase full of different shoes. It was the task of the selected lady to try them on and to parade up and down in front of him until he reached a climax.

The forms and fashions of shoes can thus differ according to the different inclinations. One person is especially enchanted by pumps, another by riding boots, a third only reacts to lace-up boots or little button-up booties, others love only dancing shoes or slippers. Hirschfeld mentions a man who was only sexually aroused by the folds around the ankles. The smell of leather is often significant as well.

Masochistic and sadistic notions frequently are part of a shoe fetish: to imagine being stepped on or kicked or to have a foot placed on one's neck.

50. 'La Goulu' and Valentin 'the Boneless', photo, 1892.

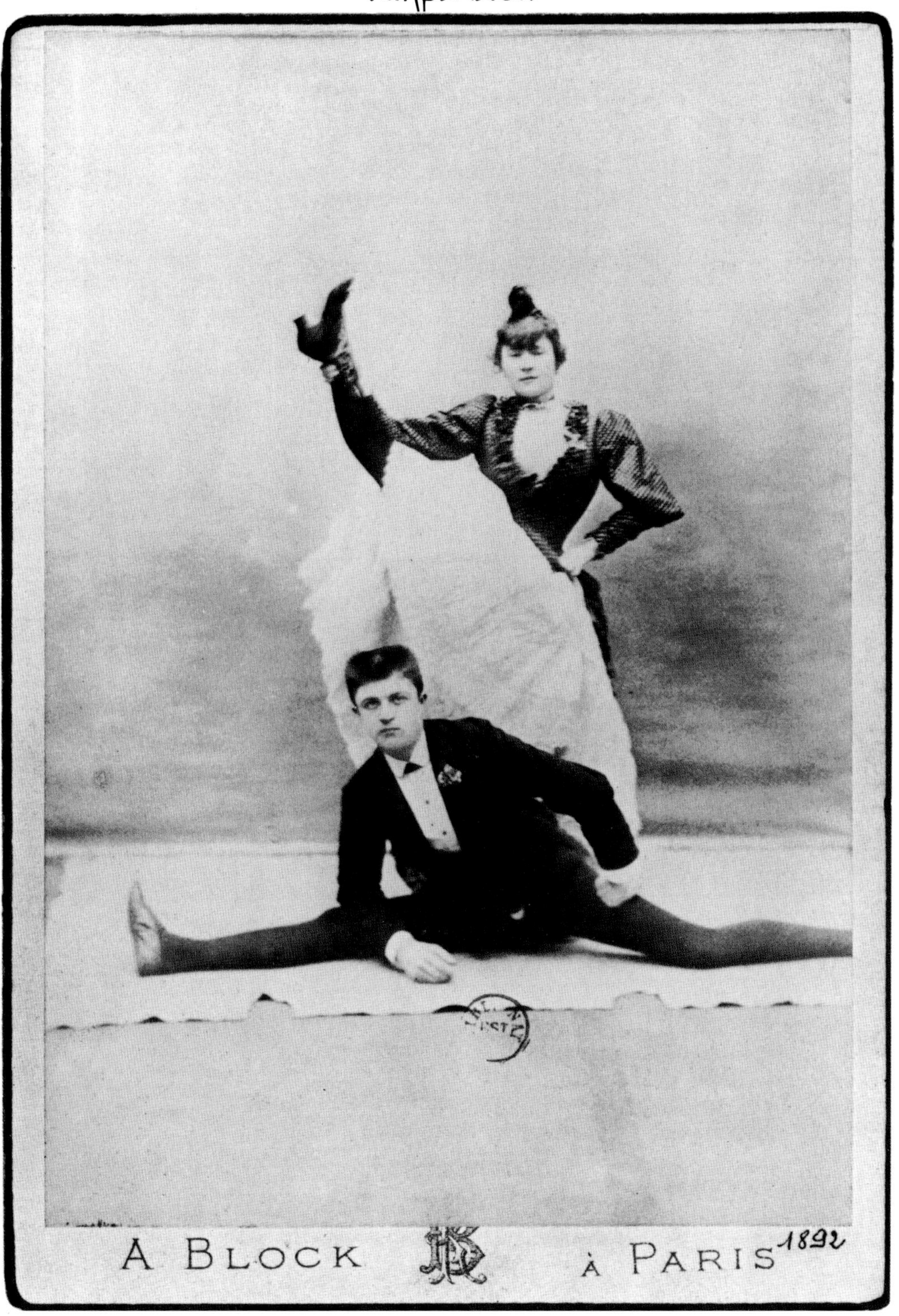
1892
A BLOCK   à PARIS

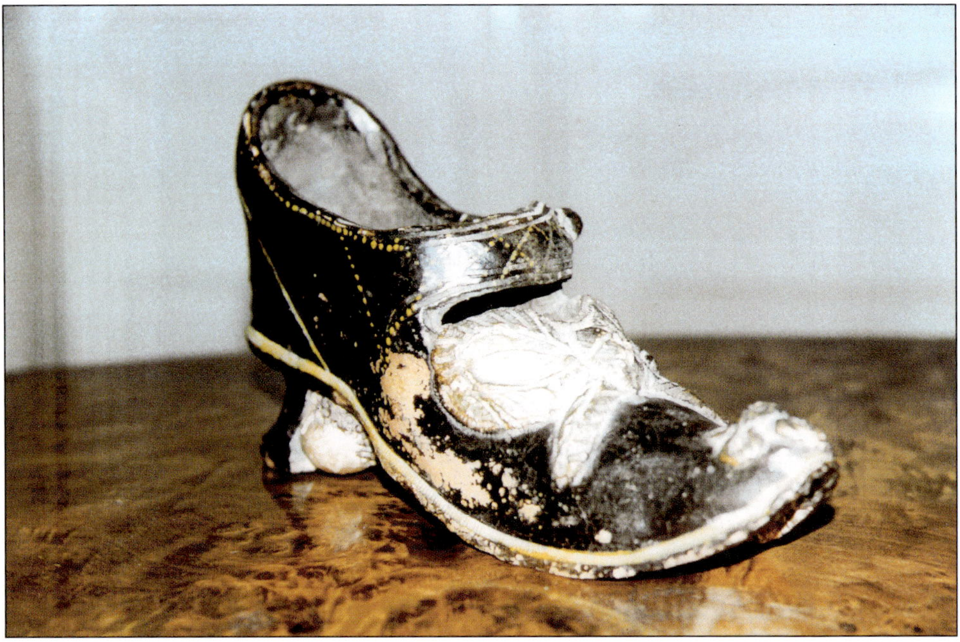

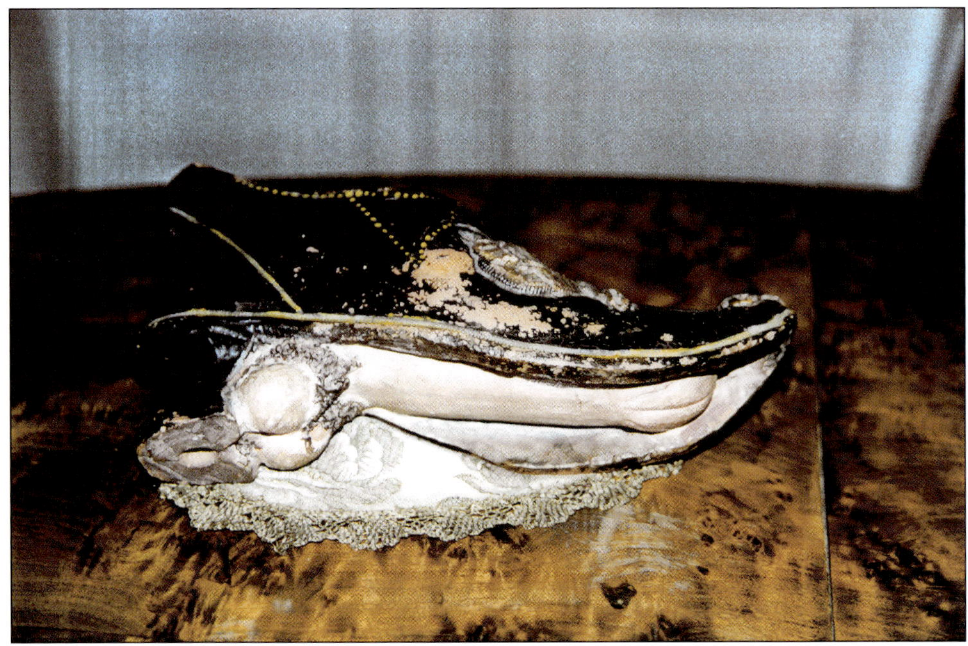

Krafft-Ebing saw in the shoe and foot fetishist a masked masochist. He assumed that foot and shoe are turned into a fetish because they symbolize the wish for being submissive or overpowered. This corresponds, perhaps, to the sign of subjugation practiced in history where the winner places his foot on the body of the loser, although in our case love would be the motive.

Entering the keyword "foot fetish" into any of the Internet search engines yields a surprising number of pages dedicated to this passion.

An internal drive therefore still exists, which keeps this fetish alive and well. However, today it has probably lost its societal and legal dramatics. Anybody is permitted to find happiness according to his or her inclinations without being labeled as "sick" as previous sexology textbooks used to do.

It is an ice-cold Easter, and I am listening to the processions of the "Semana Santa" [Holy Week] in Seville on a Spanish radio station. How much bloody, chain-rattling masochism and seemingly medieval terror and naïve worship of relics is hidden in these rituals!

51, 52. Shoe with a penis embedded in the sole, terracotta, around 1750.

The "Hermandades" [brotherhoods] are very
popular. Even women establish sisterhoods that
participate in the processions. The need for
transcendence increases.
As far as that is concerned, the foot and shoe
fetish is only a secular variation of a religious
ritual of veneration that has slipped completely
into the private realm. It guarantees the same
passionate impetuses and edifications. Fetishism
– an ardent, poetic private religion in a religious
time?

53. Anonymous photo dating from 1890–1900.

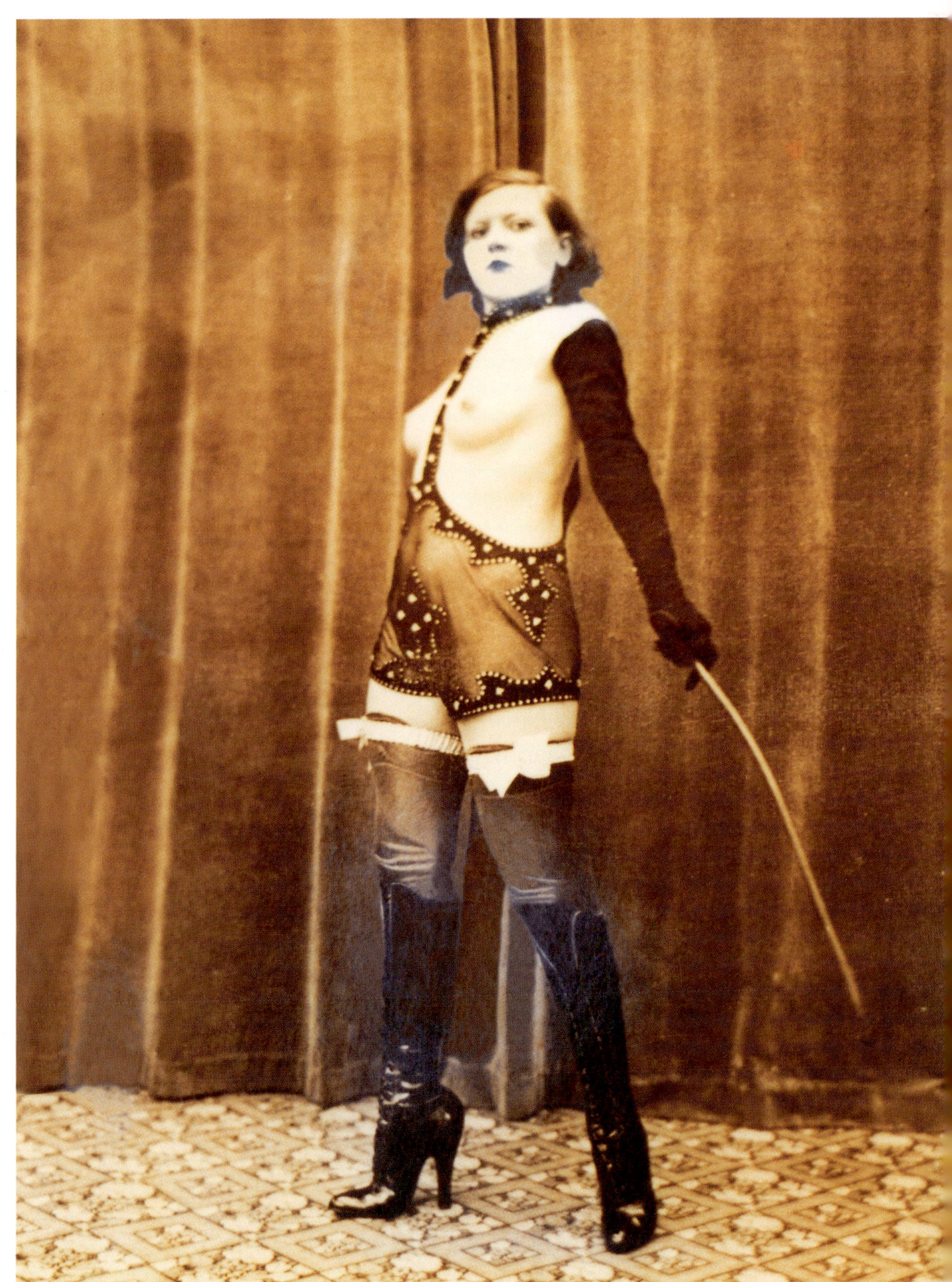

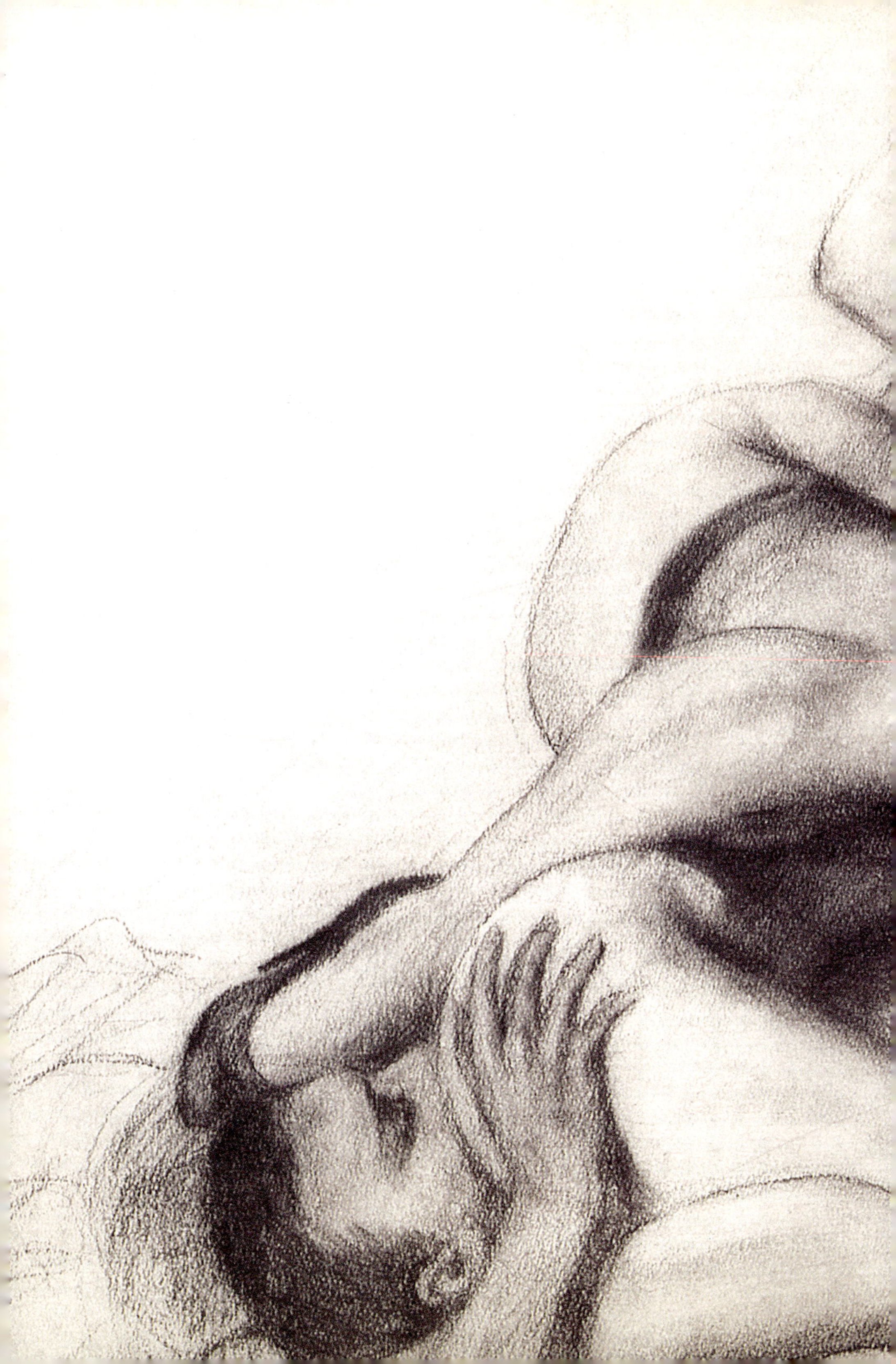

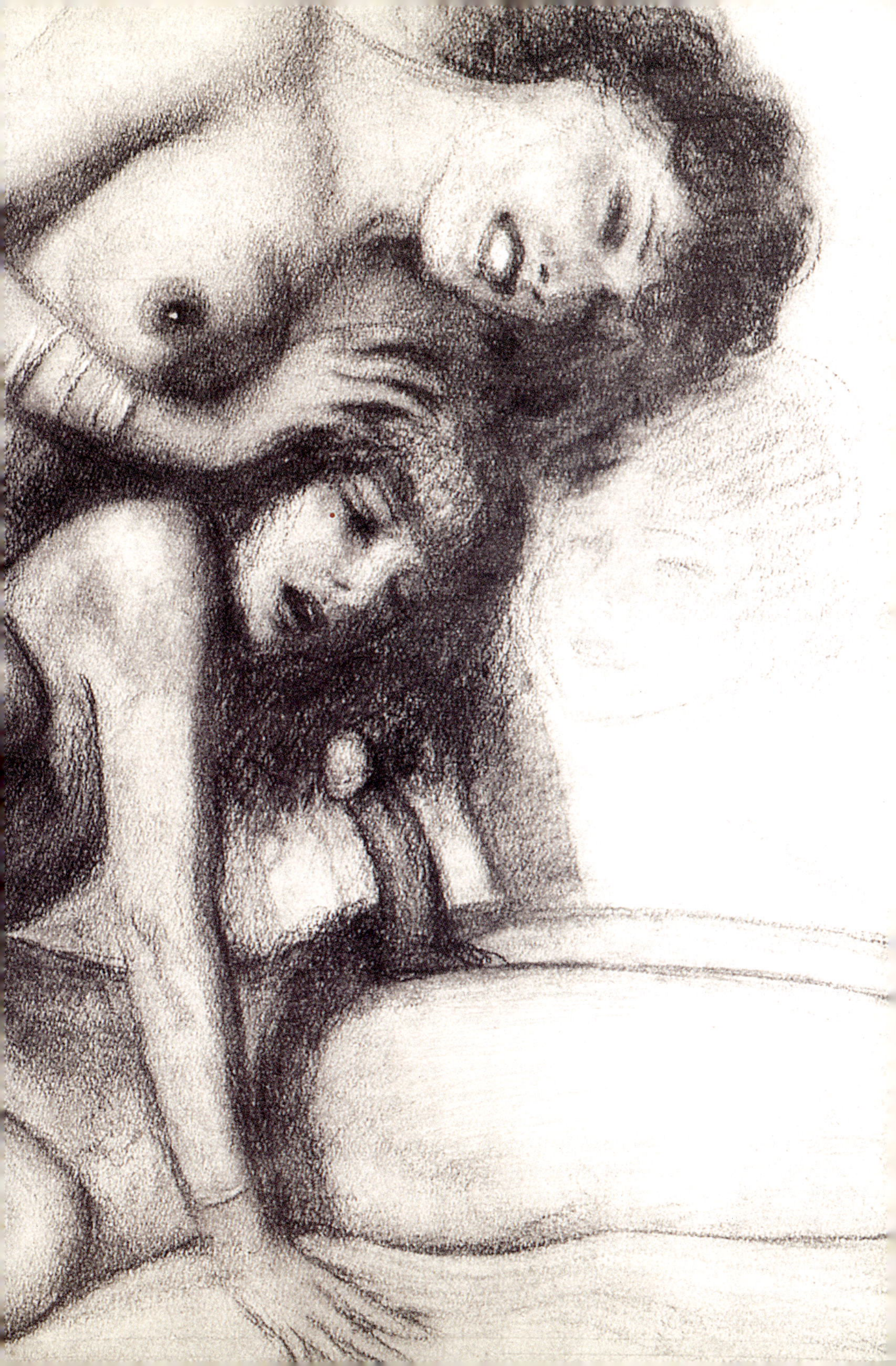

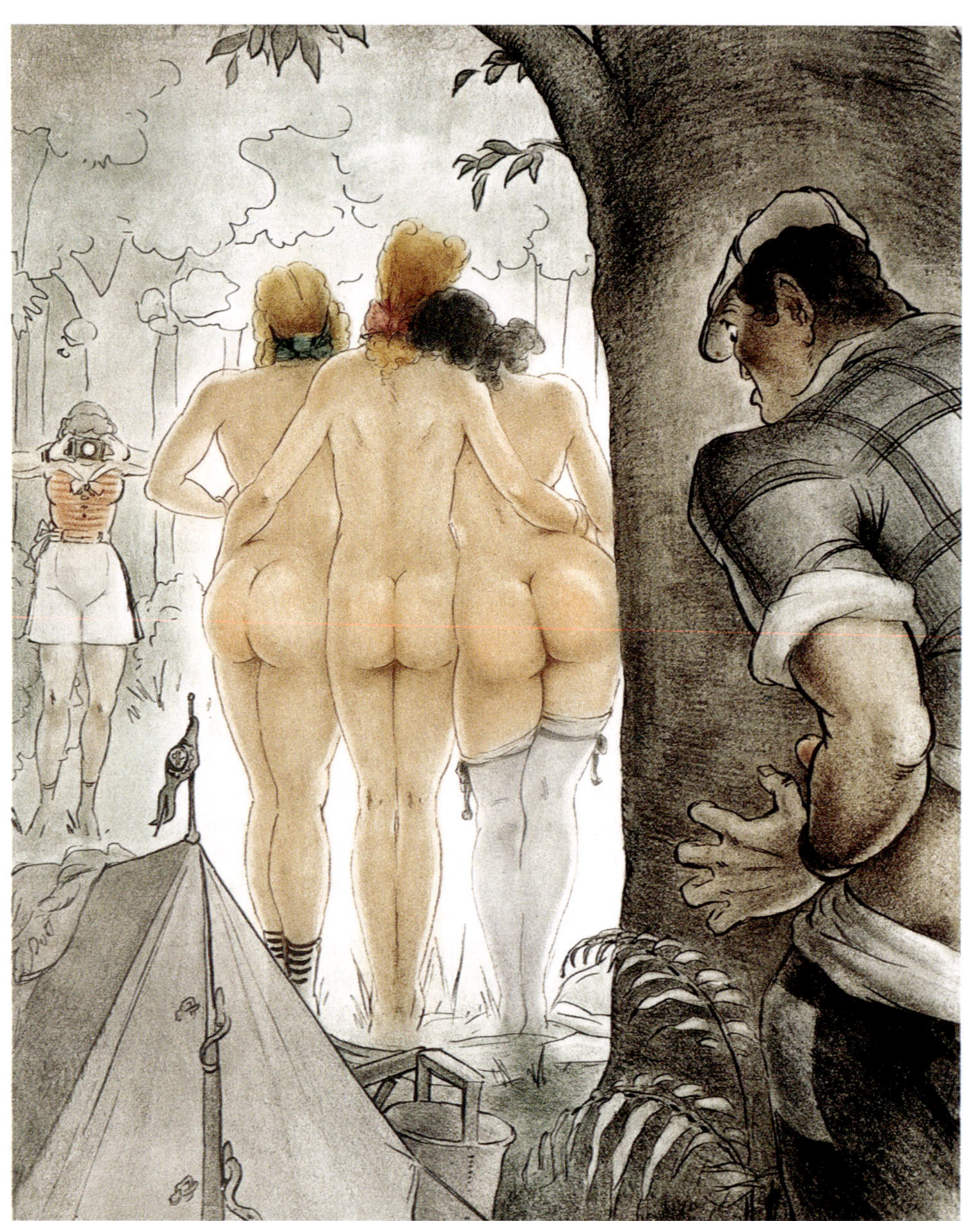

Preceding Pages :
54. Marcel von Herrfeldt, lithograph.
55. Jean Morisot, colour engraving, around 1925.
56. Félicien Rops, Pornocrates, 1878.

Temptation

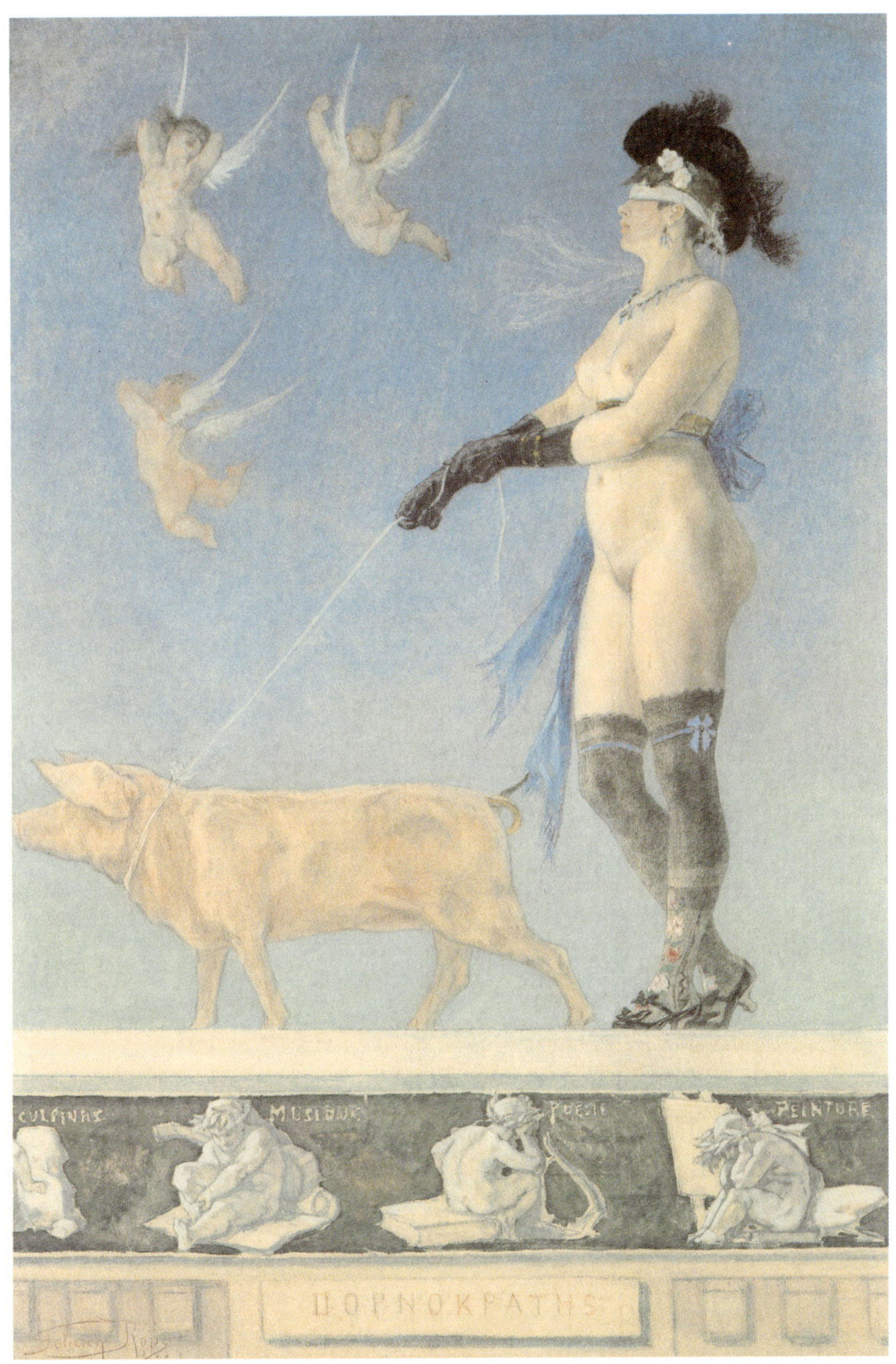

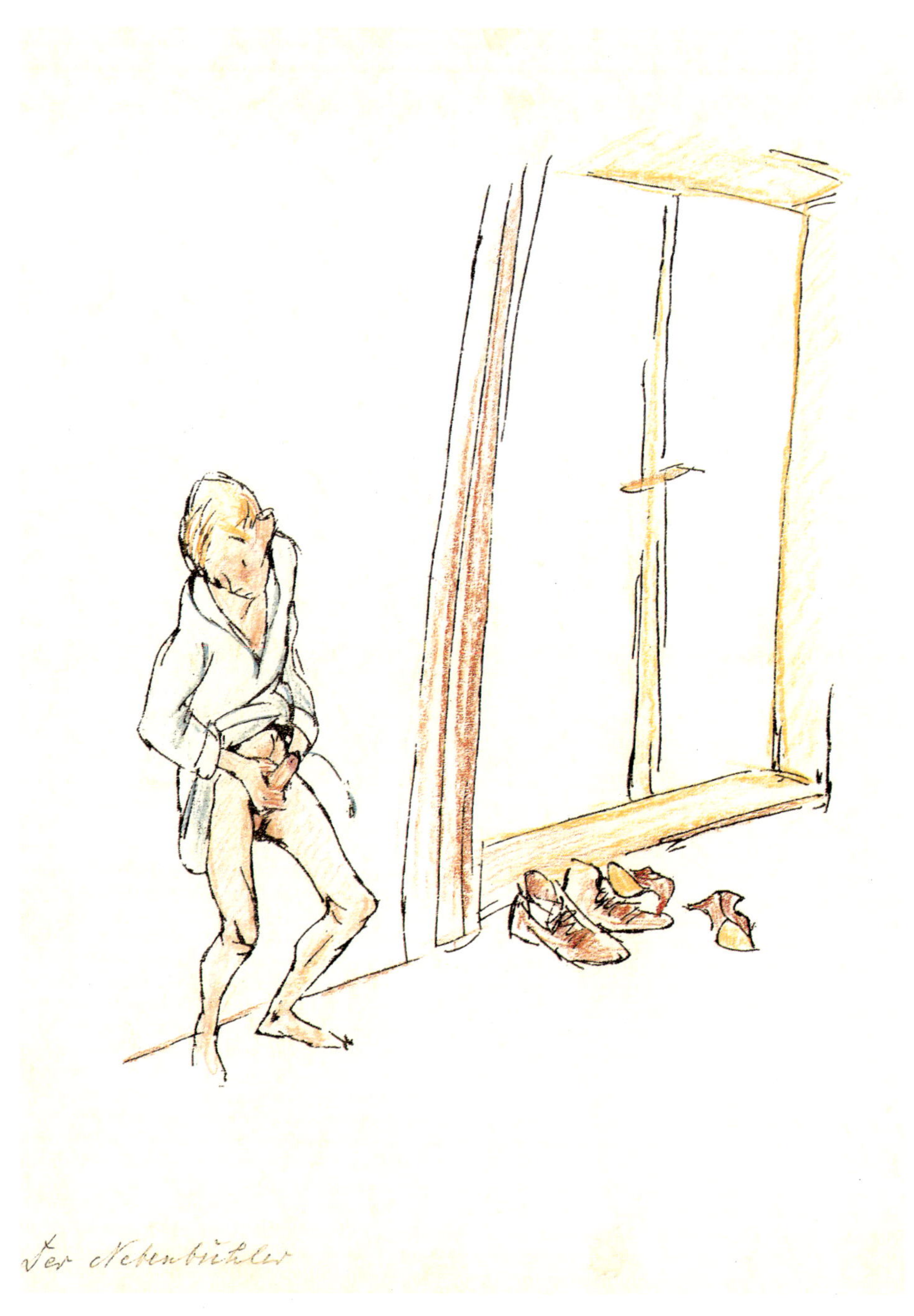

57. The Rival.

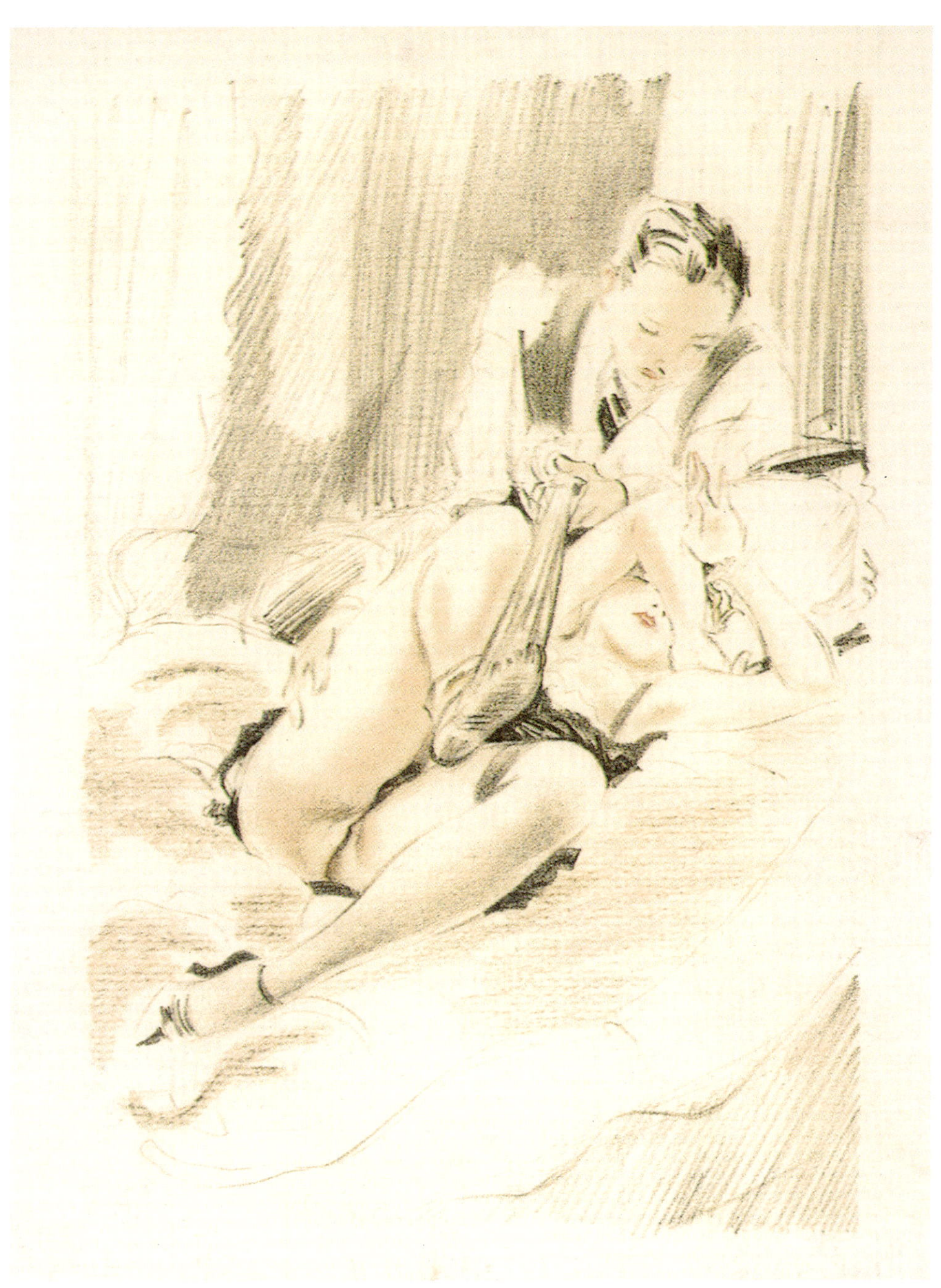

58. Rojan, Springtime Idyll, 1933.

Captions

1. Watercolour, from an English notebook, 1880.
2. Rojan, Voyeurs, around 1930.
3. Photo of a young Parisian girl, around 1900.
4. Photo, Paris, around 1900.
5. Léon Bakst, La Sultane Jaune, 1916.
6. Valentin Serov, Portrait of the Princess Olga Orlova, 1911.
7. Zinaïda Serebriakova, Dancer's Dressing-room: Snow Crystals, 1923.
8. De Monceau, watercolour, around 1940.
9. Léon Bakst, costume design for Potiphar's wife, La Légende de Joseph, 1914.
10. Egon Schiele, The Green Stocking, 1914.
11. Gustave Courbet, Woman in White Stockings, 1861.
12. Giorgione, Judith, around 1500.
13. François Boucher, La Toilette (detail), 1742.
14. Otto Schoff, colour lithograph, around 1930.
15. Anonymous, Venus, Goddess of Love, 17th century.
16. Anonymous design dating from the 1950s, Germany.
17. Rojan, watercolour, 1925.
18. Rojan, Voyeurs, around 1930.
19. Rojan, Voyeurs, around 1930.
20. Egon Schiele, Portrait of the Artist's Wife Holding Her Right Leg, 1917.
21. Rosarium Philosophorum, Les Très Riches Heures du Duc du Berry, 1556.
22. Cold-painted bronze dating from the end of the 19th century.
23. Photo, Paris, early years of the 20th century.
24. Orgiastic Dream, lithograph.
25. Anonymous French etching, 1910.
26. Antoine Watteau, Diane au Bain, 1712.
27. Rojan, watercolour, 1925.
28. Rojan, In the Taxi, watercolour, 1930.
29. Otto Schoff, lithograph, around 1930.
30. Anonymous drawing, 1922.
31. Fashion-design, Perugia, 1920s.
32. Margit Gaal, lithograph, 1921.
33. Peter Paul Rubens, The Meal at the House of Simon the Pharisee, around 1620.
34. Edgar Degas, Dancer Adjusting Her Shoe, 1880–1885.
35. Henri de Toulouse-Lautrec, Nude Study, 1883.
36. Couple in Natural Surroundings, watercolour, American, 1930s.
37. De Monceau, watercolour, around 1940.
38. Joe Brockerhoff, aerograph.
39. Joe Brockerhoff, aerograph.

40.   Joe Brockerhoff, aerograph.
41.   Jean Morisot, colour engraving, 1925.
42.   Egon Schiele, Woman in Black Stockings, 1913.
43.   Wedding book, probably Japanese, 19th century.
44.   Wedding book, probably Japanese, 19th century.
45.   Coloured shunga ('Images of Spring'), silk on card, 18th century.
46.   Coloured shunga ('Images of Spring'), silk on card, 18th century.
47.   Woman's shoe, London, 1720.
48.   Anonymous etching, Paris, around 1920.
49.   Boot with laces, 1890.
50.   'La Goulu' and Valentin 'the Boneless', photo, 1892.
51, 52. Shoe with a penis embedded in the sole, terracotta, around 1750.
53.   Anonymous photo dating from 1890–1900.
54.   Marcel von Herrfeldt, lithograph.
55.   Jean Morisot, colour engraving, around 1925.
56.   Félicien Rops, Pornocrates, 1878.
57.   The Rival.
58.   Rojan, Springtime Idyll, 1933.

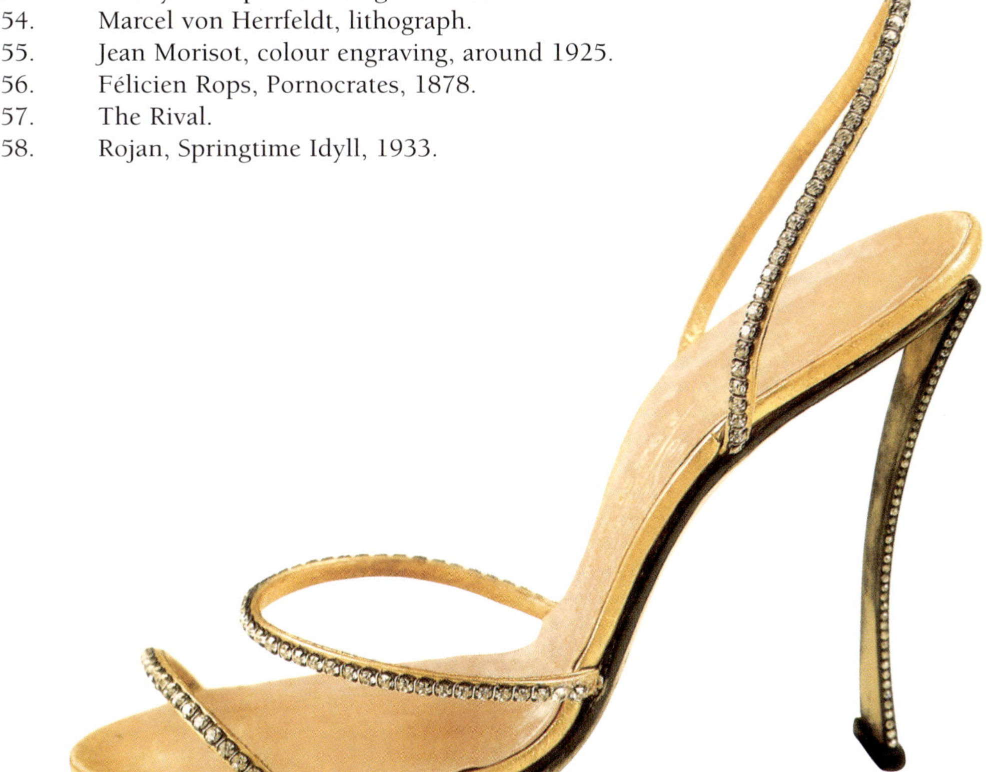